BONANZA:
THE DEFINITIVE
PONDEROSA
COMPANION

BY MELANY SHAPIRO

Thanks . . .

. . . to Mom, Dad and Marc for this wonderful instrument of destruction, my workstation.

. . . to Jonathan, my compassionate husband and merciless editor.

. . . to the next generation (in progress) for keeping it all in perspective.

. . . to everyone else (too numerous to mention) who has offered support and encouragement. Special thanks to the *Bonanza* mailing list for all the great conversation, not to mention the hundreds of answered questions.

Dan Blocker college photos/documents appear courtesy of the Archives of the Big Bend, Bryan Wildenthal Memorial Library, Sul Ross State University, Alpine Texas.

ISBN #1-890723-18-5
Library of Congress Cataloging-in-Publication Data
Melany Shapiro

    Bonanza: The Definitive Ponderosa Companion

    1. Bonanza: The Definitive Ponderosa Companion (television, popular culture)
I. Title

Published by Cyclone Books, 420 Pablo Lane, Nipomo, CA 93444. Email: cyclone@lightspeed.net

First Printing 1997

Printed in Hong Kong

TABLE OF CONTENTS

An early publicity photo of David Dortort's Cartwright clan.

The Founding of the Ponderosa

Nearly half a billion people have enjoyed *Bonanza* through the years. Few of them realize that this golden vision of family, decency, and the American west, was created for just one purpose - to sell color TVs.

NBC's parent company, RCA, had made huge strides in color technology by September, 1959. But most consumers weren't ready to invest in another contraption; less than 5% of the U.S. population owned a color set. There just weren't enough color shows. So NBC was ordered to spare no expense in producing a pioneer color program, and they turned to veteran novelist and producer David Dortort to create the concept. Dortort had the experience they needed, and he was a firm believer in another exciting new concept – the hour-long show.

Bonanza's concept was born quickly, according to Dortort. "[A] Comstock lode story told from the point of view of the Cartwrights — a father and three sons whose allegiance is not to silver but to the land. The three sons are forever at each other's throats, but when the chips are down they forget their differences and fight shoulder to shoulder."

Dortort's also wanted to fight what he called "Momism". Sitcoms of the 1950's, he felt, damaged the father image. "Father always turned out to be a fool," he explained, "On TV it's mother who really knows best. Ben Cartwright is not a blithering idiot, but someone his three sons can respect." His choice of Lorne Greene for Ben could not have been better — throughout his career on *Bonanza* and after, Greene received thousands of letters from misunderstood teenagers idolizing him as the perfect father figure.

Trouble in Virginia City

NBC had great confidence in Bonanza. Production costs were nearly $100,000 a week — one of the highest to that point. Yet even with a seasoned producer, brilliant color, and an astro-

nomical production cost, *Bonanza* almost didn't make it. NBC showed the program on Saturdays at 7:30PM, when many people shopped in department stores and could see color televisions on display. But the home audience was already hooked on CBS' *Perry Mason*.

The reviews were no help. Americans couldn't walk down the street in the late 1950s without stepping in a western – thirty others debuted almost simultaneously. *Bonanza*'s September 12 premiere inspired this *Variety* review:

> *Another western is just what Saturday night television needs least, and that's what Bonanza appears to be — just another western. For all its pretensions, with a large cast, name guests, color and an hour's length, proves to be little more than a patchwork of stock oater ideas without a fresh twist to distinguish it...*

"We were almost off before we went on," Lorne Greene said years later. "We were shooting our sixth show when the scuttlebutt was that the man with the sharpened pencil at NBC in New York said our show cost too much, and that it should end after 13 episodes."

Late in the first season, a rumor was printed that the show **was** actually canceled. A flood of mail poured in, and for the first time NBC knew *Bonanza* had an audience. While still not a huge success, the show was saved.

The Legend Endures

The big break came in 1961, at the start of *Bonanza*'s third season. NBC moved the Cartwrights to Sunday at 9PM, and it is in this time period that most fans remember the show today. *Bonanza* ruled Sunday night for a decade, and won over the world. At the show's peak, 480 million viewers in 97 countries called the Cartwrights their friends. And thanks to the wonder of reruns, we will always bring the Ponderosa into our homes and hearts.

Lorne Greene: Pa

He was the bonding force of the Ponderosa, the burly man with the deep voice and the wisdom of the ages. Without him, his sons would have lived their lives in stupor, Virginia City would have burned to the ground, and NBC would have lost their women 40-and-older demographics. He was patriarch Ben Cartwright, ideally portrayed by Lorne Greene.

Greene was born February 12, 1915, in Ottawa, Ontario, Canada, the only surviving child of Russian-Jewish immigrants Daniel and Dora Greene. Lorne enjoyed a fine relationship with his parents and based Ben Cartwright on his father, a stern but gentle man who made orthopedic shoes and boots (the younger Greene was named after his first customer, Lorne MacKenzie). In later years Lorne Greene described his father as a man who "didn't have to punish; all he had to do was look. He had almost perfect control, never got excited. Like Ben, he thought things through," he said. "I don't know whether I could ever match my father as a person," he told the New York Post in 1964, "but as an actor I try to be like him."

In high school at The Lisgar Collegiate Institute, Lorne's booming voice got him a part in the French comedy Les Deux Sourds as one of two deaf characters who shout at each other throughout the production. He was instantly hooked on acting. Lorne attended Queen's University in Kingston, Ontario, from 1932 to 1937 and was active in the drama guild producing, directing and acting in many productions. He changed his major from chemical engineering (which he had pursued to please his father) to French and German languages to have more time for acting, though Queen's University had no drama major at the time.

Lorne maintained a close relationship with Queen's University through the years and was awarded an honorary doctorate in 1971. His convocation speech had some fatherly advice for the graduating class: "get yourself a really comfortable bed and a really good pair of shoes, because you're going to be in one or the other for the rest of your life." He asked one of the professors, "am I really referred to now as 'Doctor?' Does that mean that my sons on *Bonanza* now call me Dr. Pa Cartwright?"

The Voice of Canada

After graduation Lorne went to New York to accept a fellowship to the Neighborhood Playhouse School of the Theatre. While in New York he also trained in stage movement at the Martha Graham School of Contemporary Dance. After two years Greene returned to Canada but found

Lorne Greene performing in "The Secret" at Queen's University, 1937 Photo courtesy Queen's University

few opportunities for actors, especially after World War II broke out. He made just $10 a week as program supervisor at an ad agency until his big baritone voice, described later as the "voice with the built in cello," landed him a job with the Canadian Broadcasting Corporation. He read the national news each night, and since the news at that time was so vital it was broadcast in every public place throughout the country. Lorne became known as "the voice of Canada," and in 1942 he became the only Canadian ever to win the National Broadcasting Company's radio award for announcing.

Later in the war Greene served overseas in the Royal Canadian Air Force. He continued his radio career in Toronto after the war, where he founded the Academy of Radio Arts to train students in broadcasting. The academy saw over 400 graduates, including Leslie Nielsen. The two became great friends, and after Greene's death in 1987 Nielsen recalled their friendship as "...a friendship without making judgments, and it's the kind of friendship, of course, that endures, and I loved him for it." Greene also co-founded the Jupiter Theatre, a repertory group with which he worked as an actor or director in over fifty productions.

To this point Lorne's work in television was limited to occasional jobs as commercial or documentary narrator. His break came by accident. Greene was also an inventor, and in the spring of 1953 he flew to New York to show an invention to NBC executives — a stopwatch that ran backwards as an aid to radio announcers. While at NBC's headquarters he met with Fletcher Markle, a Canadian producer who had taught at Greene's radio academy. Markle was producing *Studio One*, a top-rated CBS dramatic anthology series. Greene then appeared in two *Studio One* programs: *Arietta*, where he portrayed an ailing orchestra conductor, and George Orwell's *1984*, where he portrayed a Thought Police official. His role in *1984* won him praise from critics and Hollywood and Broadway producers, and led to his Broadway debut as a suave radio journalist in

The Prescott Proposals. Lorne returned to Canada in the summer of 1955 to appear as the Prince of Morocco in *The Merchant of Venice* and as Brutus in *Julius Caesar*.

Stardom was nearly his. Throughout the mid-1950's Greene appeared in dozens of films and television shows including *Tight Spot* (Columbia, 1955), *Peyton Place* (Twentieth Century Fox, 1957), *Driftwood* (*The Elgin Hour*, ABC, 1955) and *Othello* (CBS). He also appeared the short-lived English television series *Sailor of Fortune*. His 1959 *Wagon Train* appearance, in which he dominated series star Ward Bond, caught David Dortort's eye. And so Lorne Greene, a Jewish Canadian who had ridden a horse just once, was cast as great American frontiersman Ben Cartwright, the patriarch of the Ponderosa.

From Despot to Dad

The first season, which lost the ratings war to *Perry Mason*, portrayed Ben as a Bible-thumping, gun-wielding old coot who threatened to shoot anyone who set foot on Ponderosa land — male or female, armed or unarmed. He even kept his three sons at arms length. Lorne Greene can be largely credited for *Bonanza*'s success, for it was he who changed Ben Cartwright from a tyrant to the father millions of viewers grew to love. In 1960 he threatened to quit over the issue. Greene's observations made sense — why would viewers care around a man who was cold to his sons and prohibited visitors? Would he shoot **all** the guest stars?

And so David Dortort remodeled Ben Cartwright, bringing his age from 65 to Greene's own age — about 50. "Acting involves asking yourself, 'What would I do in this situation?'" Greene told Look magazine in 1964, "So when I come in 8 a.m. for work, I don't turn into someone else." Ben became kinder, both to his sons and Ponderosa visitors. *Bonanza* focused less on defending the Ponderosa and more on relationships. In the process it found its niche. *Bonanza* was no longer just another western, it was a warm program about family and personal justice.

Of the four principle actors, Greene identified with his character the most — it was often said that he had become Ben Cartwright. He built an exact model of the Ponderosa ranch house in Mesa, Arizona, complete with the famous staircase to nowhere. Offscreen, he offered fatherly advice to Dan Blocker and Michael Landon; the three of them entering into several successful land ventures together. When he wasn't filming *Bonanza*, Greene made public appearances in character at rodeos and in Las Vegas nightclubs. A typical public appearance would consist of a grand entrance in costume followed by a little song:

> *I'm an old cowhand*
> *From TV Land*
> *And my dapple gray*
> *Is a Chevrolet*

He'd then tell corny one-liners about Little Joe and Hoss. "Little Joe thought the three R's meant ridin', ropin' and rasslin'. Hoss? He got an A in one subject — lunch. His favorite four-letter word? Food. He got his best marks in geography...Turkey, Sandwich Islands. There were no free-dirty-speech movements in those days. We didn't even have PTA. What we did have was PTAH — Pa takes a hand."

A Man Who Loved his Work

"The illusion is everything," Greene told Look magazine. "*Bonanza* gives pleasure to millions of people, and it has provided a roof over the heads of all those. If [this article] damages it by going in too deep, by saying that we're just actors, not anything like the Cartwright family, you may sow the seeds of the show's death."

What did Lorne Greene, a man who had known success as a Shakespearean actor, think of *Bonanza*'s quality? "Look, nobody claims that every script we do is great," he told Look magazine, "If we get eight or ten good ones out of 34 in a year, that's a lot more good theater than there would be

without *Bonanza*." Unlike Pernell Roberts, Greene reconciled his feelings. "He prefers acting in Shakespeare or something else that's been filtered through three hundred years of great minds," he said after Roberts' departure from *Bonanza*. "I love it too. But when you do a new show every six days, some things are not possible."

Although Greene enjoyed worldwide success (at its height, *Bonanza* was enjoyed in 97 countries), nowhere was his popularity greater than his native Canada. In 1965 he was named Canadian Man of the Year, an honor usually bestowed upon prime ministers and war heroes. In March of that year each of his nine appearances at the Canadian Western Exposition in Edmonton, Alberta, sold out, despite snow, sleet and sub-zero temperatures.

The father of all father figures -- Lorne Greene as Ben Cartwright

Lorne also enjoyed a successful recording career, using his commanding baritone to sing and tell stories of the old west. In 1962, along with Pernell Roberts, Dan Blocker and Michael Landon, he recorded *Ponderosa Party Time*, and the 1964 holiday season saw *Christmas at the Ponderosa*. He also released a number of wonderful solo albums, including *Welcome to the Ponderosa*, which includes the *Bonanza* theme and *Saga of the Ponderosa*.

Bonanza was canceled in January, 1973, after a fourteen-year, 430-episode run. A philosophical Lorne Greene commented in a *Daily News* interview, "No program should last on television for more than five years. There are far too many people around with so many great ideas who would never see the light of day if we didn't move on and make room for them." After *Bonanza*, he appeared as a private-eye in the short-lived series *Griff*, as Captain Adama in *Battlestar Galactica*, as an arson investigator in 1984's *Code Red*, and as a dog-lover in Alpo commercials where his line, "That's 105 to you and me," is nearly as memorable as Ben Cartwright's, "Let's ride!" He also did numerous guest appearances — twice reunited with his television sons. He appeared with Pernell Roberts in the 1978 season premiere of *Vegas*, and with Michael Landon in a 1984 episode of *Highway to Heaven*. Greene was looking forward to filming *Bonanza: The Next Generation* when his health began to fail. Dortort revised the script several times to make the role less physically demanding, but Lorne Greene never lived to see production. He died on September 11, 1987, of pneumonia following surgery for a perforated ulcer, and with his death the world mourned the loss of the Western's greatest "Pa."

Film and Television Credits

Studio One, "Rendezvous" (CBS, 6/1/53)
Othello (1953)

Studio One, "A Handful of Diamonds" (CBS, 4/19/54)
You Are There "The Fall of Parnell" (CBS, 6/13/54)
Studio One "The Cliff" (CBS, 9/13/54)
The Silver Chalice (1954)

You Are There "The Torment of Beethoven" (CBS, 1/2/55)
Climax "Private Worlds" (CBS, 4/7/55)
Star Stage "The Toy Lady" (NBC, 9/9/55)
Studio 57 "Death Dream" (SYN, 11/13/55)
Tight Spot (1955)

Alfred Hitchcock Presents "Help Wanted" (CBS, 4/1/56)
Alcoa Hour "Key Largo" (NBC, 10/14/56)
Armstrong Circle Theater "Flareup" (NBC, 10/30/56)
U.S. Steel Hour "Survival" (CBS, 11/7/56)
Autumn Leaves (1956)

Producers Showcase "Mayerling" (NBC, 2/4/57)
Kraft Television Theater "The Medallion" (NBC, 4/3/57)
Playhouse 90 "Edge of Innocence" (CBS, 1957)
Studio One "Twenty-Four Hours to Dawn" (CBS, 11/11/57)
Sailor of Fortune (series) (SYN, 12/27/57)
Peyton Place (1957)

Shirley Temple's Story Book "The Little Lame Prince" (NBC, 7/15/58)
The Buccaneer (1958)
The Gift of Love (1958)
The Last of the Fast Guns (1958)

Gale Storm Show "Jailmates" (CBS 2/28/59)
Wagon Train "The Vivian Carter Story" (NBC, 3/11/59)
Cheyenne "Prairie Skipper" (ABC, 5/5/59)
Mickey Spillane's Mike Hammer "A Haze on the Lake" (SYN, 7/7/59)
My True Story (episode title unknown, NBC, 7/25/59)
Bonanza (series) (NBC, 9/12/59 to 1/16/73)
The Trap (1959)

Here's Hollywood (NBC, 1960)
The Third Man "The Hollywood Incident" (NN, 1960)
Cheyenne "Gold, Glory and Custer - Part I" (ABC, 1/4/60)
Cheyenne "Gold, Glory and Custer - Part II" (ABC, 1/11/60)

The Errand Boy (1961)

Perry Como's Kraft Music Hall (NBC, 1962)

The Andy Williams Show (NBC, 1963)
The Art Linkletter Show (NBC, 1963)
The Tonight Show Starring Johnny Carson (NBC, 1963)
Missing Links (NBC)

Lorne Greene with Brian Keith in "Tight Spot", 1955. Leonard Maltin gives this film 3 1/2 stars!

What's This Song? (NBC, 1964)

Allan Sherman's Funnyland (NBC, 1965)
ABC Nightlife (ABC, 1965)

The Dean Martin Show (NBC, 1968)
The Merv Griffin Show (SYN, 1968)
The Joey Bishop Show (ABC, 1968)

Dinah Shore Special (NBC, 1969)
Jimmy Durante Presents the Lennon Sisters Hour
  (ABC, 1969)
Destiny of a Spy (TV movie) (NBC, 10/27/69)

Movin' (NBC, 1970)

The Harness (TV movie) (NBC, 11/12/71)

A Salute to Television's 25th Anniversary (ABC, 1972)

Griff (series) (ABC, 9/29/73 to 1/4/74)
Nippon Chinbotsu (1973)

The Merv Griffin Show (SYN, 1974)
Sandy in Disneyland (CBS, 1974)
Rex Harrison's Short Stories of Love "The Fortunate
  Painter" (NBC, 5/1/74)
Earthquake (1974)

Nevada Smith (TV movie) (NBC, 5/3/75)
Man on the Outside (TV movie) (ABC, 6/29/75)

Tattletales (CBS, 1976)
The Moneychangers (miniseries) (NBC, 12/4, 5, 12, 19 '76)

Roots (miniseries) (ABC, 1/24, 1/25/77)
SST - Death Flight (TV movie) (ABC, 2/25/77)

Hardy Boys/Nancy Drew Mysteries "The Hardy Boys and
  Nancy Drew meet Dracula" (ABC, 9/11, 9/18/77)
Happy Days "Fonzie, the Movie Star?" (ABC, 9/13/77)
The Trial of Lee Harvey Oswald (TV movie)
  (ABC, 9/30, 10/7/77)

The Bastard/Kent Family Chronicles (TV movie)
  (SYN, 5/22, 5/23/78)
Mission Galactica: The Cylon Attack (1978)
Battlestar Galactica (series) (ABC, 9/15/78 to 4/29/79)

The Love Boat "The Wedding" (ABC, 9/15/79)

Galactica 1980 (series) (ABC, 1/27/80 to 5/4/80)
Vegas "Aloha, You're Dead" (ABC, 11/5/80)
    Note: Pernell Roberts also appeared in this episode.
A Time for Miracles (TV movie) (ABC, 12/21/80)
Klondike Fever (1980)

Aloha Paradise (ABC, 2/25/81)
Code Red (TV movie) (ABC, 9/20/81)
Code Red (series) (ABC, 11/1/81 to 3/28/82)

Police Squad "A Substantial Gift" (ABC, 3/4/82)
The Love Boat "Love Will Find a Way" (ABC, 11/20/82)
Ozu no Mahotsukai (Wizard of Oz) (1982)
  (voice, U.S. version)

Highway to Heaven "The Smile in the Third Row"
  (NBC, 11/20/85)

The Canadian Conspiracy (MAX, 1986)
Vasectomy: A Delicate Matter (TV movie) (1986)

The Alamo: Thirteen Days to Glory (TV movie)
  (NBC, 1/26/87)

Pernell Roberts: The Dark Cartwright

"I feel like I'm an aristocrat in my field of endeavor," Pernell Roberts said in a 1965 interview, just after his last season. "My being part of *Bonanza* was like Isaac Stern sitting in with Lawrence Welk."

Confessing later that *Bonanza* was not what he thought it was when he signed his contract, Pernell Roberts hated the show almost from the beginning. He felt the scripts appealed to a low mentality and accused NBC of producing mediocrity while avoiding controversy. He said starring on *Bonanza* was hard on his conscience. Dubbing the show a "reprehensible lie," he was infuriated that *Bonanza* glorified the wealthy when poverty was widespread. He also objected to the objectifying of women, pandering to women's fantasies of being carried off by a Cartwright.

Roberts tried for years to cancel his *Bonanza* contract. Threatened by NBC executives that he would never work there or anywhere else again, he completed his six-year contract (1959-1965) by walking through his part. He told reporters he never read the scripts; he just said whatever lines he was told to. Yet the producers insisted he was doing a great job. "Those silly asses," Roberts said, "You give them one tenth of what a scene requires and they think its great."

Roberts has defied establishment his entire life. He was born in Waycross, Georgia, on May 18, 1928, the son of a soft-drink salesman. His poor discipline caused him to flunk out of college three times, once at Georgia Tech and twice at the University of Maryland. He served two years in the Marines between schools.

At the University of Maryland Pernell took up acting. Roberts appeared in four plays at the University theater, then went to summer stock in Cleveland and to Washington DC's Arena Theatre, where he appeared in (appropriately) *The Firebrand*. After two years with the Arena group he did minor productions in New York and Wisconsin. He eventually won a part in Broadway's

The Lovers with Joanne Woodward. The Broadway appearance led to film work in *Desire Under the Elms* (Paramount, 1957). This brought him to David Dortort's attention.

The Bad Boy of the Ponderosa

Roberts' defiant attitude on the set earned him the nickname "the bad boy of the Ponderosa." He called the closeness of the Cartwright family a fraud and complained that he was playing only "one-fourth of a character." A director once found him drawing heavy black lines through a script, claiming he was "trying to get some honesty into it." The antagonism between he and his costars was no secret, especially his problems with Michael Landon. "You can imagine how it is for an actor to be delivering his lines and get nothing but a blank stare from the person he is talking to," Landon said. "...Pernell said he only gave 10 percent of his creative effort to the show. Well, maybe 20 percent would have helped us a little more."

In an interview immediately after leaving *Bonanza*, Roberts gave Landon an extremely backhanded apology. "When he asked why I wanted to leave the show, I told him," Roberts said. "I pointed out that there was not an equality of competence among the actors, that he himself was untrained, that he was perpetuating bad acting habits. I meant all this constructively. I was trying to convey that he was not getting the fullest potential from his talent. I was attempting to say that he wasn't developing himself. Somehow he took it as a personal attack. He never forgot. I'm sorry."

Roberts' (usually female) fans adored his dark, brooding presence, so much so that he usually got more fan mail than any of his three costars. Although he left in disgust less than half way through *Bonanza*'s run, he left behind episodes that, despite his opinion, remain classics to his fans.

One of Roberts' best was *The Crucible*, guest-starring Lee Marvin, which aired April 8, 1962. Adam is robbed in the desert while on his way to a few days rest after a cattle drive. The two outlaws take $5,000 and his horse, leaving Adam stranded in the desert without food or water. Near death, he stumbles upon a lonely prospector named Kane (Marvin) who gives Adam food and water and offers to loan him a mule and enough supplies to reach civilization in exchange for three days' work in a gold mine. Adam has no choice but to agree, but soon discovers Kane is a madman determined to prove that, with enough torture, Adam can be driven to kill him. Kane kills the mule and forces Adam to be his pack animal, even tying him up at night with the same rope used to tie the mule. Finally, after bearing more torture than any normal human being could take (he was a Cartwright, after all) Adam cracks, wrestles Kane to the ground and starts strangling him, until Kane manages to squeeze out a feeble "I win, I win." Adam, ashamed that he was nearly driven to kill, puts the injured Kane on a stretcher and begins to drag him toward civilization. Meanwhile, Ben, Hoss and Little Joe, about to abandon their two-week search and begin mourning, find a delirious Adam dragging a dead man through the desert. The reunion of the four Cartwrights still brings tears to viewers' eyes, over 35 years later.

The (Almost) Married Cartwright

In 1964, to appease Roberts, David Dortort was prepared to make an exception to the Cartwrights' eternal bachelorhood. He planned to have Adam marry a young widow named Laura Dayton. If Roberts left at the end of the season, marriage would be a convenient way to write him out. On the other hand, the added dimension to his role might entice him to stay.

But the outspoken actor was years ahead of his time. In one of his last suggestions to NBC, Roberts asked for Adam's bride to be a Native American played by a black actress. "Recent events in the South have done tremendous damage to our national prestige and have clearly indicated the grievous wrong that has been perpetrated upon American Negroes," he wrote. "I have found this to be tremendously distressing, embarrassing and humiliating, as a man, as an American and as a Southerner." His letter continued, "It seems to me that the forthcoming addition to the format of *Bonanza*, the impending marriage of Adam Cartwright, offers an unparalleled opportunity which might help toward the rebuilding of our national image and integrity...[This] would be one of the most progressive and constructive statements in television drama, as both the Negro and the American Indian have constantly been exploited 'second class citizens'. ..."

NBC thanked him for the letter and said that "the part would be cast in consideration of all the requirements necessary for the role." Later, Dortort said he thought the suggestion was "well meaning, but confused." "To ask a Negro to play an Indian doesn't solve anything," he said. "It is an empty gesture toward civil rights." He pointed out that Sammy Davis Jr. was slated to guest star in an upcoming episode (although he never did). He also cited the planned episode *Enter Thomas Bowers*, about a black opera singer suspected of being a runaway slave. But for Adam's bride, blonde, blue-eyed Kathie Browne was chosen. Roberts' idea was just too radical for 1964.

Kathie Browne as Laura Dayton appeared in four melodramatic episodes. In *The Waiting Game*, Laura's husband dies in a horse accident. We discover Laura had secretly despised her husband for years and wished him dead. When her wish comes true, she feels guilty, realizing how much her daughter, Peggy had adored her father. Her longtime friend Adam comforts Laura and a romance begins. In the next two episodes, *The Cheating Game* and *The Pressure Game*, we see the ups and downs of their relationship, culminating in Adam's tender proposal following Laura's near-death in an accident.

Dortort was correct to test the waters before allowing a Cartwright marriage. After these episodes were aired NBC was swamped with letters from female fans insisting all four Cartwrights remain unmarried. Pernell Roberts was forced to stay another year and scriptwriters had to undo Adam marriage plans. In her fourth and final episode, *Triangle*, Laura feels neglected when Adam spends long days away from her, refuses to tell her what he's doing, and spends their evenings together asleep on the couch. Laura falls in love with Adam's cousin, Will Cartwright (Guy Williams , of *Zorro* and *Lost in Space*). Laura and Will look for Adam so they can break the news and discover why he has been so secretive, and why he has fallen asleep every evening. He has been building a house, his own Ponderosa for him and Laura. As if that weren't enough, Adam falls off the roof and is paralyzed from the waist down. Laura, out of guilt, vows to marry Adam, yet he refuses to let his paralysis stand in Laura and Will's way. He pushes himself up from his wheelchair, takes a few steps, and gives Laura and Will his

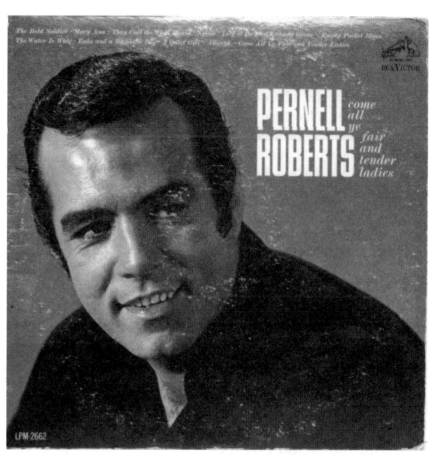

A surprisingly good collection of folk music from 1963. Available on the Bear Family CD box set.

blessing. The happy couple rides off, never to be seen again, Adam limps into the house, and viewers are treated to one more year of four bachelor Cartwrights. Everyone is happy except Pernell, trapped in the "fairytale kingdom."

During the filming of *Triangle*, Look magazine's Senior Editor John Poppy witnessed the filming of that final scene. Roberts began pushing himself up from the wheelchair, but the director felt he was coming up too fast. "Hold it longer," the director said. "Show more suffering as you push with your arms."

"Gentlemen," Roberts responded, "my legs are damaged, not my arms. I'm supposed to be a big strong man, and there is no reason for me to have trouble doing a little push-up like this. I'll suffer when I'm on my feet, if you don't mind."

The director insisted, and Roberts gave up his fight. John Poppy described it like this:

He began to push with his arms, setting his face in an expression that made me whisper, 'My God, what is it?' It was remarkable. Roberts radiated suffering, bravery, strain and a nearly tearful look of hurt plus something else that might have been pain or mockery. At length, he heaved himself upright and swayed out of camera range. I relaxed as his face went blank, but he startled me by clearing his throat loudly and loosing a great spit. Right on the porch of his Pa's house.

Pernell Roberts left *Bonanza* at the end of the 1965 season without a farewell episode; occasionally it was mentioned later that Adam had gone to California, back east, Europe or the sea. His departure from the show is considered among the worst mistakes in television history, comparable only to McLean Stevenson's departure from *M*A*S*H*. Lorne Greene urged him to stay, take his fortune (in 1965 he was earning $10,000 per episode, plus residuals) and buy his own studio where he could produce more "worthwhile" programs. But immediately after his departure Roberts told reporters he wouldn't go back for a million dollars. "I have only one life not to waste," he said. He incorrectly assumed his *Bonanza* fame would put him in demand for more significant roles. Instead, he was forced to take any role available, including dinner theater, summer stock, and guest appearances on *Marcus Welby*, *Perry Mason* and, ironically, *Gunsmoke*. His more permanent return to television wasn't until 1979, in CBS' *Trapper John, M.D.*, a part which he took "to raise money for the mortgage." He hated that show also, but stayed with it until its end in 1986. Since then, *Bonanza*'s sole survivor has appeared in commercials and on ABC's *FBI: the Untold Stories*. He refuses to discuss *Bonanza*.

Film and Television Credits

Gunsmoke, "How to Kill a Woman" (CBS, 11/30/57)
Cheyenne, "Misfire" (ABC, 12/10/57)

Trackdown, "The Reward" (CBS, 1/3/58)
Have Gun - Will Travel, "Hey Boy's Revenge" (CBS, 4/12/58)
Zane Grey Theater, "Utopia Wyoming" (CBS, 6/6/58)
Shirley Temple's Storybook, "Hiawatha" (NBC, 10/5/58)
Northwest Passage, "The Assassin" (NBC, 11/16/58)
Zane Grey Theater, "Pressure Point" (CBS, 12/4/58)
The Sheepman (1958)

Sugarfoot, "Most Wanted" (ABC, 2/18/59)
Lawman, "The Posse" (ABC, 3/8/59)
Alcoa Presents One Step Beyond, "The Vision" (ABC, 3/24/59)
Bronco, "The Belles of Silver Flats" (ABC, 3/24/59)
77 Sunset Strip, "Abra Cadaver" (ABC, 4/17/59)
Bonanza (series) (9/12/59 to 5/23/65)
Ride Lonesome (1959)

The Detectives, "House Call" (ABC, 1/29/60)

The Errand Boy (1961)

Naked City, "The S.S. American Dream" (ABC, 5/8/63)

Route 66, "Child of the Night" (CBS, 1/3/64)

The Girl from Uncle, "The Little John Doe Affair" (NBC, 12/13/66)
The Virginian, "Long Journey Home" (NBC, 12/14/66)

Big Valley, "Cage of Eagles" (ABC, 4/24/67)
Carousel (special) (ABC, 5/7/67)
Wild Wild West, "Night of the Firebrand" (CBS, 9/15/67)
Mission: Impossible, "Operation…Heart" (CBS, 10/22/67)
Gunsmoke, "Stranger in Town" (CBS, 11/20/67)

Ironside, "To Kill a Cop" (NBC, 1/25/68)
Big Valley, "Run of the Cat" (ABC, 10/21/68)
Mission: Impossible, "The Mercenaries" (CBS, 10/27/68)

Name of the Game, "Chains of Command" (NBC, 10/17/69)
Lancer, "Welcome to Genesis" (CBS, 11/18/69)
The Silent Gun (TV movie) (ABC, 12/16/69)
Four Rode Out (1969)
The Kashmiri Run (1969)

Mission: Impossible, "Death Squad" (CBS, 3/15/70)
San Francisco International (TV movie) (NBC, 9/29/70)

Bold Ones: The Doctors, "A Matter of Priorities" (NBC, 1/3/71)

Alias Smith and Jones, "Exit from Wickenburg" (ABC, 1/28/71)
Hawaii Five-O, "The Grand Stand Play" (CBS, 3/3, 3/10/71)
Name of the Game, "Beware of the Watchdog" (NBC, 3/5/71)
Men from Shiloh, "Wolf Track" (NBC, 3/17/71)
Marcus Welby, M.D.. "The Tender Comrade" (ABC, 9/14/71)
The Bravos (1971, TV movie)

Night Gallery, "The Tune in Dan's Café" (NBC, 1/5/72)
Alias Smith and Jones, "21 Days to Tenstrike" (ABC, 1/6/72)
The Bravos (TV movie) (NBC, 1/9/72)
The Adventure of Nick Carter (TV movie) (ABC, 2/20/72)
Assignment: Munich (TV movie) (ABC, 4/30/72)
Owen Marshall, Counselor at Law, "The Trouble with Ralph" (ABC, 10/19/72)
Sixth Sense, "I Did Not Mean to Slay Thee" (ABC, 11/11/72)
Banacek, "To Steal a King" (NBC, 11/15/72)

Marcus Welby, M.D., "The Day After Forever" (ABC, 2/27/73)
Mission: Impossible, "Imitation" (CBS, 3/30/73)
Mannix, "Little Girl Lost" (CBS, 10/7/73)

Hawkins, "Candidate for Murder" (CBS, 3/5/74)
Police Story, "Chief" (NBC, 3/19/74)
The Odd Couple, "Strike Up the Band or Else" (ABC, 10/17/74)
Nakia, "Roots of Anger" (ABC, 11/30/74)

Police Story, "To Steal a Million" (NBC, 2/4/75)
Dead Man on the Run (TV movie) (ABC, 4/2/75)
Medical Story, "Test Case" (NBC, 9/25/75)
The Deadly Tower (TV movie) (NBC, 10/18/75)
Ellery Queen, "The Adventure of Colonel Niven's Memoirs" (NBC, 10/23/75)
The Lives of Jenny Dolan (TV movie) (NBC, 10/27/75)
Bronk, "Deception" (CBS, 12/7/75)

Cannon, "House of Cards" (CBS, 1/14/76)
Six Million Dollar Man, "Hocus Pocus" (ABC, 1/18/76)
Jigsaw John, "Death of the Party" (NBC, 3/22/76)
Captains and the Kings (1976, miniseries)

Barnaby Jones, "Testament of Power" (CBS, 1/20/77)
Switch, "Camera Angles" (CBS, 1/30/77)
Baretta, "The Reunion" (ABC, 2/2/77)
Quincy, M.E., "Visitors in Paradise" (NBC, 2/18/77)

Most Wanted, "The Driver" (ABC, 3/14/77)
Police Woman, "Deadline Death" (NBC, 3/22/77)
Streets of San Francisco, "Breakup" (ABC, 5/12/77)
Feather and Father Gang, "The Golden Fleece" (ABC, 5/21/77)
Charlie Cobb: Nice Night for a Hanging (TV movie) (NBC, 6/9/77)
Westside Medical, "Risks" (ABC, 6/30/77)
Man from Atlantis, "Shoot-Out at Land's End" (NBC, 11/8/77)

Rockford Files, "The House on Willis Avenue" (NBC, 2/24/78)
Wide World of Mystery, "Alien Lover" (ABC, 3/29/78)
Hardy Boys/Nancy Drew Mysteries, "Arson and Old Lace" (ABC, 4/1/78)
Hardy Boys Mysteries, "Assault on the Tower" (ABC, 10/15/78)
Quincy, M.E., "Death by Good Intention" (NBC, 10/26/78)
Centennial, "For as Long as the Water Flows" (NBC, 11/4/78)
Vegas, "Milliken's Stash" (ABC, 11/8/78)
Centennial, "The Massacre" (NBC, 11/11/78)
The Immigrants (TV movie) (SYN, 11/20, 11/21/78)
The Magic of Lassie (1978)

The Paper Chase "A Case of Détente" (CBS, 4/17/79)
Night Rider (TV movie) (ABC, 5/11/79)
Hot Rod (TV movie) (ABC, 5/25/79)
Trapper John, M.D. (series) (CBS, 9/23/79 to 9/4/86)

Vegas, "Aloha, You're Dead" (ABC, 11/5/80)
    Note: Lorne Greene also appeared in this episode.

Pernell Roberts, wishing his contract were in the path of that axe

The Love Boat (ABC, 11/15/80)
High Noon, Part II: The Return of Will Kane (TV movie) (CBS, 11/15/80)

Battle of the Network Stars (ABC, 11/20/81, 5/7/82)
Incident at Crestridge (TV movie) (CBS, 12/29/81)

Hotel (pilot episode) (ABC, 9/21/83)

Circus of the Stars (special) (CBS, 12/8/85)

National Geographic, "Realm of the Alligator" (special, narrator) (PBS, 4/17/86)

Desperado (TV movie) (NBC, 4/27/87)

Night Train to Kathmandu (TV movie) (DIS, 6/5/88)

Around the World in 80 Days (miniseries, 1989)
Perry Mason: The Case of the All-Star Assassin (1989)

Checkered Flag (TV movie, 1990)
Donor (TV movie, 1990)

FBI: The Untold Stories (series, host, 1991)

Dan Blocker maintained a close relationship with Sul Ross State College (now called Sul Ross State University). This appearance is from the early years of Bonanza.

Dan Blocker: The Gentle Giant

"My dad used to say I was the onliest man in Texas that wears a No. 14 plus shoe and a size 3 hat," Dan Blocker told the Texas Standard-Times in 1963. "He also said that I was too big to ride and too little to hitch to a wagon — no good for a damned thing."

His father was wrong. For thirteen glorious years viewers loved Blocker's giant presence in their homes. At six-foot-four and nearly 300 pounds, with a smile as big as he was, Dan Davis Blocker as Hoss Cartwright continues to charm audiences over twenty-five years after his passing.

Weighing 14 pounds at birth, Blocker was the biggest baby ever born in Bowie County, Texas. Football was a natural – at 12 years old Dan was six feet tall and weighed 200 pounds! In his teens Blocker distinguished himself as an outstanding lineman and the best fighter in O'Donnell, Texas. Every Saturday night, residents roped off a section of Main Street and pitted Blocker against opponents twice his age. He never lost.

BIG Man on Campus

Blocker's life changed while attending Sul Ross State College in Alpine, Texas. The head of the drama department, Annie Kate Ferguson, needed someone strong enough to drag bodies out of the basement during *Arsenic and Old Lace*. The football team's biggest lineman was the natural choice. Thinking that drama did not fit his image, Blocker took the part only because he was pursuing a woman in the drama department. Ferguson became ill and Freda Gibson-Powell, a former Sul-Ross student, took over the production. Powell encouraged Blocker to choose the stage over football.

Although their relationship changed the course of television history, Sul-Ross folklore says the first time they met Powell threw Blocker out of the auditorium for heckling actors. Thank goodness their subsequent meetings went better.

With Powell's encouragement, there was no pulling Dan off the stage. The charismatic giant even convinced his football teammates to try acting. He directed a production of *Mr. Roberts* with every team member in the cast. "After that," he recalled in TV Guide, "I couldn't get those guys off my back. They all wanted to be actors."

GOLD KEY — BONANZA — 12¢

BONANZA

A ghost comes back to claim the lives of his alleged slayers— THE CARTWRIGHTS!

Blocker changed his major from physical education to drama. He developed a love of Elizabethan theater, and his performance as Othello (with a heavy coat of Max Factor #14) was praised. His most notable performance at Sul Ross was also in blackface, as De Lawd in *Green Pastures*. That role won him the 1949 Best College Acting award. Faculty member Dr. Noble Armstrong wrote, "...What fortuitous circumstances combined to produce that most appropriate selection of Dan Blocker to play the pontifical role of De Lawd. Compelling indeed were his majestic physique, his gigantic stride, magnificent stage bearing, mellifluous voice, convincing gestures, and most of all, his inimitable 'natural' Negro dialect..." A young girl with a small part in *Green Pastures* was also impressed, the diminutive Dolphia Lee Parker of Alpine, Texas, the future Mrs. Blocker.

In 1950, Dan did stock theater at Boston's Brattle Hall Theatre and appeared on Broadway in *King Lear*. Success seemed to be coming quickly until he was drafted into the Korean War and nearly died on Christmas Eve, 1951. Blocker later said his brush with death drove him into introspection, away from acting. He left the service and married Dolphia in 1952. Dan then taught sixth grade while working toward his Masters degree in Shakespeare at Sul Ross. Although he loved teaching, he left that career and his home state in 1956 to resume acting.

Blocker enjoyed success over the next two years in guest appearances in shows like *The Rebel* and *Gunsmoke*. Because of his enormous size and gruff voice, he was always the heavy. In 1957, tired of the stereotype, he nearly left acting to go back to teaching, until David Dortort cast him as a sympathetic deaf mute in *Restless Gun*. Blocker's performance confirmed Dortort's hunch, that Dan was capable of far more than dim-witted heavy roles, and Dortort cast him in the role that made him a legend.

No Ma'am, not Horse, Hoss

Hoss' character really emerged in *Bonanza*'s third episode, *The Newcomers* (September 26, 1959) where he falls in love with Emily Pennington, a young woman with a respiratory disease. We see not only the ex-lineman beating up the woman's evil fiancé, but Hoss' gentle side as he cares for Emily on the long trail. He carries her when she weakens and cheers her with tales of blooming dogwood trees.

Hoss' kind and caring nature brought him added responsibility. In *Tax Collector* (1961) Hoss must deliver two species simultaneously. A horse is on the stable floor, a woman is in bed, and kind, gentle, petrified Hoss runs from one to the other. The scene is hilarious and touching.

The comedic episodes almost always relied on Blocker. *Hoss and the Leprechauns* (December 22, 1963) is still a St. Patrick's Day tradition among stations that carry *Bonanza*. While fishing, Hoss sees "the littlest fellers" he's ever seen, a band of tiny men dressed in green. He tries to convince his family and the townspeople that he really did see little green men, with a sincerity that was ole Hoss' trademark. After some ridicule, a visiting Irishman tells Hoss and the townspeople about Leprechauns; if a leprechaun is captured he will hand over a strongbox full of gold to his captor, since leprechauns treasure freedom more than gold. Virginia City goes wild at the news and storm the Ponderosa. After several hours of shouting "Here, leprechaun, leprechaun, leprechaun," the townspeople go home, leaving Hoss alone to search, more to erase shame than to get the gold. He finally traps a leprechaun in a tree but three others sneak up on him, one atop the other (atop the other), and knock him unconscious. Ben, Adam and Little Joe, worried because it just wasn't like Hoss to miss a meal, ride out to find him sleeping sweetly. Hoss explains to his disbelieving family that he was attacked by little green men. This time, however, he is saved; all four Cartwrights spot the leprechauns. A hilarious slapstick fight follows, after which the Cartwrights learn that the little green men are circus performers working for the exploitive Irishman. As in all comedies, there is a happy ending. The Irishman is run out of town, Ben lets the men keep the gold they had mined on Ponderosa land, and Hoss delivers a classic speech to all Virginia City encouraging them to welcome Virginia City's newest settlers.

Another wonderful Hoss comedy is 1967's *Maestro Hoss*, guest-starring Zsa-Zsa Gabor. A gypsy named Madame Marova (Gabor) tells Hoss he is a musical genius. By an amazing cooincidence the $178.50 Hoss had earned from selling two of Pa's horses is the exact price Marova is charging for an old fiddle she calls a Stradivarius. Convinced he is a great maestro who will perform for kings and queens, Hoss practices day and night, much to the dismay of Ben, Little Joe, Hop Sing, the ranch hands, and assorted farm animals. Little Joe tells Hoss straight out that he bought an old fiddle. Hoss gets defensive, "This ain't no fiddle, it's a Stradivarius." Joe: "What in the world is a Stradivarius?" Hoss: (pause) "Well, there was a violin maker named Stradi and he made various violins and this is one of 'em."

Beyond Hoss Cartwright

Blocker's comedic timing arose from a lifelong sense of humor. His college roommate, Gene Hendryx, told a Sul Ross newspaper that living with him for four years was a "constant comedy" and an ongoing joke battle. Hendryx considered himself victorious when, after Dan and Dolphia left for their honeymoon, he broke into their apartment and filled their bathtub with $70 worth of red gelatin. "It was during the cold months and it firmed up quite nicely...In fact, by the time Dan and Dolphia returned, a green mold had developed on the red stuff," he recalled. Refusing to accept defeat, Dan tried to hire a concrete firm to pour cement in his former roommate's bathtub. When they refused, Blocker simply trashed his friend's apartment while Hendryx and his wife were out of town.

He played a simpleton on TV, but in reality Dan Blocker was an intellectual and an accomplished political speaker

Even during the height of stardom, Blocker never forgot the home folks. During a public appearance in 1964 at the State Fair in Lubbock, he held an open house at his motel and issued radio broadcasts inviting old friends to join him for a party. He stocked three hotel suites with cases of whiskey and Lone Star non-pasteurized draft beer — Dan loved his bourbon and beer. For three nights, after his 15-minute appearances, he partied with kinfolk, Korean-war buddies, promoters, college classmates and local dignitaries. "Dan's not concerned with any formalities," explained Lev Davis, another former roommate. "If the governor's waiting downstairs and a dude comes to the door whom he hasn't seen in ten years, he'll see the dude first."

At the same time Hoss Cartwright was asking "What do we do next, Paw?" Dan Blocker was married with four children: twins Danna and

Debra, and two sons, David and Dirk. The Blockers lived in a comfortable but simple Early-American home in the San Fernando Valley, their one luxury being a twelve-foot deep swimming pool — large enough for the man of the house. Blocker thought it worth the long commute to escape what he called the "snobbery" of Beverly Hills and to give his family some privacy. Privacy was a losing battle for the Blockers; Dan often complained that he couldn't even treat his children to ice cream sodas without a public spectacle, and his presence at school functions created a mob scene. At times he even wished he hadn't left teaching. "I still can't believe that people are that interested in me," he told TV Guide in 1964, "If they don't have anything more to concern them than Hoss Cartwright, then what hope is there? You know, if Dr. Salk walked down the street, nobody'd recognize him. I find that terrifying.".

Did Dan Blocker ever watch *Bonanza*, or any of the other popular shows on television? "...I don't watch this show. I don't watch any of them," he told Look magazine, "because when a writer puts a lot into building to an emotional moment, and the director, actors and technical people add all they can, and then some jackass breaks in to sell me something, it makes me MAD as hell. Pay TV is the only hope for good theater."

At the show's peak, Blocker earned over $20,000 per episode, plus residuals. In the late 1960's he and his two remaining costars sold their syndication rights for an undisclosed seven-figure sum. Among his many investments were shares in a fertilizer company, and a barbecue fuel called "Ole Dan's Mesquite Wood Chips". He also entered business ventures with Lorne Greene and Michael Landon. Despite his wealth he never forgot his roots, and never let stardom change him. A grip on the set called him "the best all-around, cotton-pickin', catch-as-catch can great guy on the lot." Offscreen, Dan held a passion for race cars and was a partner in a firm called Vinegaroon Racing Associates. He put aside all commitments to attend the Indy 500 each year, and he one day hoped to enter one of his cars in the race (he didn't do the driving; he left that to a

A natural-born comedian, Dan Blocker shows off his talents on "Laugh-In" with Goldie Hawn, circa 1969

friend). "Race drivers aren't interested in TV," he told TV Guide, "All they talk about is racing."

Blocker's other love was politics. He was such an effective political speaker that a few Texas newspapers proposed him for governor. "I would not dare run for office on the popularity of Hoss Cartwright," he told Look magazine. "Maybe I could come back [to Texas] first and teach for a while, and then run under my own name." A liberal Democrat and civil rights proponent, he campaigned for Lyndon Johnson and often found himself in segregation debates with fellow southerners. He once angered NBC officials by sharply debating Hedda Hopper, a Goldwater Republican, at a banquet thrown by General Motors, Bonanza's primary sponsor.

Blocker's biggest moment should have occurred in the two-hour episode Forever. In this show, which Michael Landon wrote for Blocker, Hoss would have finally gotten married. But his happiness would be destroyed in the second hour when his pregnant wife is murdered. Real-life tragedy intervened when Blocker died suddenly of a lung clot on May 13, 1972, age 43, during the hiatus between Bonanza's thirteenth and four-teenth seasons. Forever was filmed on schedule with Joe as the tragic groom; the script otherwise went virtually unchanged. Only a few words were said about Hoss' death; everyone sensed that Blocker would not want a memorial episode. Convinced also that Blocker would want Bonanza to go on without him, Dortort tried to keep the show alive, though he acknowledged Blocker was irreplaceable. David Canary was brought back – he had quit playing foreman Candy a year earlier to pursue a writing career – and the role of Ben Cartwright's adopted son Jamie, played by Mitch Vogel, was expanded. Tim Matheson portrayed a new character named Griff King, an outlaw who unwillingly works on the Ponderosa. Despite Dortort's efforts, Bonanza limped along for only half a season without Dan Blocker and rode into the sunset on January 16, 1973.

Film and Television Credits

Gunsmoke, "Alarm at Pleasant Valley" (CBS, 8/25/56)

Cheyenne, "Land Beyond the Law" (ABC, 1/15/57)
Sgt. Preston of the Yukon, "Underground Ambush" (SYN, 4/25/57)
Tales of Wells Fargo, "Renegade's Raiders" (NBC, 5/20/57)
Colt .45, "A Time to Die" (ABC, 10/25/57)
Restless Gun, "Jody" (NBC, 11/4/57)
Restless Gun, "The Child" (NBC, 12/23/57)
Outer Space Jitters (1957)
Girl in Black Stockings (1957)

Walter Winchell File, "The Reporter" (File #20) (ABC, 1958)
Wagon Train, "The Dora Gray Story" (NBC, 1/29/58)
Sugarfoot, "The Deadlock" (ABC, 2/4/58)
Have Gun - Will Travel, "Gun Shy" (CBS, 3/29/58)
Thin Man, "The Departed Doctor" (NBC, 4/4/58)
The Virginian, (pilot episode) (NBC, 7/6/58)
Restless Gun, "The Way Back" (NBC, 1958)
Restless Gun, "Mercy Day" (NBC, 10/6/58)
Jefferson Drum, "Stagecoach Episode" (NBC, 10/10/58)
Cimarron City, "I, the People" (NBC, 10/11/58)
Gunsmoke, "Thoroughbred" (CBS, 10/18/58)
Maverick, "The Jail at Junction Flats" (ABC, 11/9/58)
The Rifleman, "The Sister" (ABC, 11/25/58)
Restless Gun, "Take Me Home" (NBC, 12/29/58)

Desilu Playhouse, "Chez Rogue" (CBS, 2/16/59)
Bonanza (series) (NBC, 1959-1972)
Rebel, (episode title unknown) (ABC, 10/4/59)
Troubleshooters, "Tiger Culhane" (NBC, 10/9/59)

Here's Hollywood (NBC, 1960)

The Errand Boy (1961)

Perry Como's Kraft Music Hall (NBC, 1962)
Henry Fonda and the Family (CBS, 1962)

The Andy Williams Show (NBC, 1963)
Exploring (NBC, 1963)

Something for a Lonely Man (TV movie) (NBC, 11/28/68)
Lady in Cement (1968)

Laugh-In (NBC, 1969)

Cockeyed Cowboys of Calico County (1970)

Popular Boy---

Dan Blocker: Renaissance Man – From football star to debate team member, Dan loved his days at Sul Ross State College (now Sul Ross State University) and Sul Ross loved Dan.

From Jock to Actor:

Left: Dan Blocker was the biggest lineman on the Sul Ross State College football team. When the drama department needed someone to drag bodies for *Arsenic and Old Lace*, who better to fill the part? He had no interest in acting at this point.

Below is a photograph of the role that started it all.

Hometown Boy Makes Good

Right: Drama teacher Freda Powell threw Dan out of the auditorium for heckling actors. Fifteen years later, she poses with her most famous student.

Below: Dan, Congressman J.T. Rutherford (classmate and debate team member), friends Gene Hendryx and Thad Corkins in 1960 Sul Ross Homecoming Parade.

October 27, 1949

Western Costume Company
5335 Melrose Avenue
Hollywood, California

Gentlemen:

We are producing The GREEN PASTURES on November 16-17, and wish to rent a costume for De Lawd. We should like a long prince albert coat of black alpaca (or other material), black trousers, congress gaiters, with a white shirt and white bow tie, and stove-pipe hat as that specified in The GREEN PASTURES script.

The following measurements are required:

Chest	52"
Waist	42"
Ins.am	30"
Height	6'3"
Collar	18 1/2"
Suit coat size	54
Weight	285

Please confirm this order and let me know what the rental price on the above costume will be. Please note that our production dates are Wednesday, and Thursday, November 16-17. Dress rehearsal will be held November 14.

Sincerely yours,

Freda G. Powell, Chairman
Speech Department
Sul Ross State College

FGP:qpw

November 15, 1949

Western Costume Company
5335 Melrose Avenue
Hollywood 145, California

Gentlemen:

I am returning by express two pieces of the costume shipped to us for "De Lawd" in GREEN PASTURES. Both the coat and the shirt, which I am returning, are much too small. The actor who is to wear these garments if of course an unusually large young man. In an ordinary business suit he wears a size 54 suit coat which is the size we asked for when we made our order. The coat you sent is marked size 54, but is much too small in the shoulders, too short waisted, and five or six inches too short in the sleeves. Since your coat marked 54 was too small, please send whatever size will be right for the enclosed tailor's measurements from which our actor has his suits made.

A 19 shirt is the correct size for our actor in an ordinary dress shirt. We could find no size marked on the shirt you sent, but it was at least 3" too small in the neck and 3 or 4 inches too short in the sleeves, and too tight across the shoulders.

The hat, gaiters, cravat, etc. were satisfactory as to size. The trousers were not right, but our actor has a pair of his own which he can wear, and we will simply keep the pair you sent and return with the complete costume after production.

Fortunately the date for our show has been put forward to November 30, and December 1 which makes it possible for us to obtain a correction in the size of the costume needed.

Sincerely yours,

(Mrs) Freda G. Powell, Chairman
Department of Speech
Sul Ross State College

FGP:qpw

Dan Blocker in Blackface:

Left page: As the NBC wardrobe department discovered ten years later, Dan was a tough man to fit into a costume.

Left and bottom right: As DeLawd in *Green Pastures*.

Lower left: As Othello.

Michael Landon: A Television Giant Earns his Spurs as Little Joe

He started as the impetuous, sharp-shooting, fist-fighting, woman-chasing young'un of the Ponderosa, but as the years went on he matured into a careful, intelligent character. He was Little Joe, played by the king of family television, Michael Landon.

A Miserable Childhood

Landon was born Eugene Maurice Orowitz in Queens, NY, on October 31, 1936. He said in interviews that his parents, Eli Orowitz and Peggy O'Neill, had an unhappy marriage. Eli had been a writer, then a radio announcer, appearing as Mr. Emo on New York's *Lady Esther Show*. He was head of RKO Radio Pictures' East Coast publicity department, becoming the publicist for Gene Autry and other celebrities. Peggy O'Neill was a beautiful but unsuccessful Broadway showgirl.

Eli was taken with Peggy's looks, but they would soon come to hate each other. Peggy complained that she had given up a great show business career to marry a "loser" and a "nobody". She lied about her career, telling her friends and even her children that she had appeared in the Ziegfield Follies and that she was another, more famous Peggy O'Neill.

When Eugene was six the Orowitzes moved to the suburban town of Collingswood, NJ, where Eli was hired as district manager of a movie theater chain. It was a guaranteed income, but to him a giant step down in his career.

Everything appeared to be normal at 623 Newell Lake Drive. Peggy seemed like a good-natured lady who sang show tunes as she cleaned the house. She offered refreshments to the neighborhood kids and taught them to tap-dance. But Michael Landon later described his mother as "off her rocker". He remembered her telling him on his sixth birthday, "Well, now you're six and I don't like you anymore because I

don't like little boys." She devoted all her attention to her daughter Evelyn, who had her mother's beauty. Peggy entered her daughter in local beauty pageants, and Evelyn eventually became Miss New Jersey. Eugene always knew his mother needed Evelyn to make up for her own lost career.

Religion was a major problem in the Orowitz household. Michael Landon described his father as "a Jew who didn't like Catholics" and his mother as "a Catholic who definitely despised Jews." His mother claimed a priest told her she couldn't receive Holy Communion if she slept with Eli. Landon later said his parents must have slept together only twice, and he and his sister were the living proof. Peggy didn't like her son's dark, curly hair, a typically Jewish characteristic, and compared it unfavorably to Evelyn's golden hair.

Eli wasn't a religious Jew, but he wanted his only son to have a Bar Mitzvah. After the bar mitzvah, his mother pulled him aside and said, "I thought you'd like to know, son, that you are not Jewish. I haven't told you or anyone else, but when you were a baby, I took you out and had you baptized Catholic. This whole day has been a joke!"

Landon's mother frequently and flamboyantly attempted suicide. Years later, he joked, "I was ten before I knew you put anything but a head into a gas oven.". He learned not to pay much attention. "I noticed that she always had a pad under her knees so they wouldn't hurt," he said, "and the window was usually open."

Landon described one attempt when he was about ten, during a rare family vacation in Florida: "My mother went into one of her weird moods. Her eyes opened wide and she seemed to just float across the floor and out the door in her nightgown. While I was pleading with my father and sister not to argue, I looked out the window and saw my mother walking toward the water. And I knew what she was going to do, or at least try to do." Peggy walked toward the surf, and Eugene ran after her, begging her to stop. Before long, they were both nearly under the water, and Eugene couldn't swim. He hit his mother in the face as hard as he could. A combination of that and a wave knocked her over.

"I pulled her onto the beach, and sat on top of her while she was crying for my sister," he said. "I swear to God, forty-five minutes later my mother and sister were in their bathing suits playing in the sand as though nothing had happened. My father did nothing except to look pathetic. And I'm on the beach, on the water's edge, vomiting."

Eugene's terrible home life caused him to spend as much time alone as possible. He found a cave in the woods near his house, and stocked it with canned food. He ate his meals there and dreamt of escaping Collingswood and having his own family. He dreamt that everyone would communicate, be open and affectionate. Many years later, he portrayed that dream in hundreds of television programs.

Life in town was little better than life at home. There were only two Jewish families in Collingswood, and anti-semitism prevailed. Many of Eugene's peers believed Jews had horns, and they'd ask to feel the top of his head. He'd sometimes walk down the street and a carful of kids would shout "Jew bastard" out their window. Things got worse when he reached dating age. Eugene once rang a doorbell to pick up his date, only to have the girl's father slam the door in his face.

Eugene had a hereditary sleep disorder which caused him to wet the bed frequently. Peggy tried to make him stop by teasing him and calling him names. When that didn't work, she hung the stained sheets out the window for everyone to see. Many times after school, Eugene would dash up the stairs and pull them in before any of his peers noticed them.

Eugene's father also had the condition as a child, but he didn't tell his son. "My dad never told me he wet the bed until I was 19 years old," he told his pal Johnny Carson on *The Tonight Show*. "Now if he told me that when I was a little kid, I would have been thrilled. Because when you're a little guy and you wet the bed, you don't think anybody in the world wets the bed except you." In 1978, Landon took the humiliating experience and turned it into the offbeat TV movie *The Loneliest Runner*, which turned out to be yet another hit for him and NBC. More importantly to Landon, maybe the movie helped a few kids like him.

The bed-wetting stopped when Eugene was fourteen, but by then his self-esteem was "in the gutter". He tried to cover his small physique with padded sweatshirts. He was shy, had nervous tics, and made gulping noises and twitched his arms. He had been a straight-A student through the seventh grade, with a near-genius IQ, but while his teachers adored him his peers didn't. So Eugene transformed himself from nerd to troublemaker. Like the rebel he was to play in *I Was A Teenage Werewolf*, Eugene began to pick fights. He got kicked out of classes and began getting failing grades.

Eugene might never have become anything but a punk except for a strange ability he discovered late in his freshman year at Collingswood High. That spring, his gym class was introduced to javelin throwing. The runt of the class, Eugene was convinced he'd make a fool of himself - but his first toss beat his classmates' by over three feet! His coach allowed him to bring the javelin home over the summer, and he spent every spare moment perfecting his toss and strengthening his upper body.

That same summer he saw Cecil B. Demille's biblical epic *Samson and Delilah*. For the rest of his life, he associated strength with Samson-like long hair. As his hair grew his javelin tosses became better and better. He was offered numerous scholarships and settled on the University of Southern California for their excellent track and field department. Although Eugene had to repeat his sophomore year, and finally graduated 299 out of a class of 301, he was accepted.

"I really thought the rest of my life was planned," Landon said years later. "I'd spend four years in college, join the service, throw the javelin in the service, maybe even win the Olympics." After that, he felt he'd build his Olympic fame into a Hollywood career. He had been nibbled by the acting bug at thirteen when he played a Japanese houseboy in "The Bat," with the Haddonfield players near Collingswood. "For the first time, I knew the excitement of fooling an audience," he said. "They all thought I was Japanese."

But his dreams died almost instantly. He lived in a fraternity house, where he didn't fit in with his burly, crew-cut frat brothers. They didn't like Eugene's long hair, and at the first practice he beat everyone's toss by a longshot, angering them further. Soon after, his teammates jumped him and shaved half his head. They also rubbed a muscle ointment called Atomic Balm on his scrotum. Eugene was broken. He shaved the other half of his head to create a balanced cut, and his strength vanished. At the next practice, the javelin fell short time after time, and Eugene tore a ligament and developed an infection. He and USC lost interest in each other, and Eugene quit school after one semester.

Eugene's parents had also moved to Los Angeles. At one point Eugene drove his father to his old studio where Eli hoped to resume his publicity career. His old pals had refused to see him or even let him on the studio lot. Landon said years later that he remembered his father mumbling, "But they were my friends. They owed me."

Eli was forced to take the first job offered, managing a single movie theater in the Los Angeles area. Eugene made a vow to himself that he'd follow the rest of his life. "No matter what I did," he said, "I wasn't going to owe anybody a favor. And I didn't expect anything from anybody that had to do with business . . . I wasn't going to take any garbage from anybody, either."

Michael Landon - The Actor and the Man

Eugene found odd jobs loading freight cars, baby-sitting, working in a soup factory, and working in a ribbon factory. "It was just ribbons, but I wanted to make the *best* ribbon," he said later. One of his co-workers at the ribbon factory was an actor and needed a partner for a Warner Brothers audition. Eugene's part in *The Home of the Brave* called for a lot of crying, which came easy to him. Although stardom was not yet upon him, Eugene joined the Screen Actors Guild and adopted a new name - Michael Landon, which he picked out of the Los Angeles phone book. When Michael was nineteen he met twenty-six year old legal secretary Dodie Levy. He was drawn to her "built-in family" – she had a seven-year-old son named Mark - because he desperately wanted to build the kind of home he had never known. After a brief courtship, they decided to marry.

Michael's mother refused to attend the wedding, but he stopped by her house on the way to church to try to change her mind. The ensuing scene was typical: "My mother pulled a knife on me, so I called the police," he said later. "I told them I didn't want to hit her but I didn't want to get stabbed, either." When the police arrived, Peggy told them her son was mentally ill. She called the psychiatric hospital, and as Michael left with the police he heard his mother describing her son's condition on the phone.

Michael cut his ties with his mother. He became much closer to his father, especially when Eli left Peggy and moved in with Michael and Dodie. Eli told Michael he'd stayed with a woman he detested strictly for the sake of his children. Michael was determined never to do that.

Landon pursued his career. He auditioned for almost anything, even singing with Jerry Lee Lewis for a short time. He spent as much time as possible on the Warner lot, auditioning for producers on the way to their cars. A producer named Jerry Stag gave him his first chance with the lead in an episode of the anthology series *Telephone Time*, "The Mystery of Kasper Hauser", about a young boy imprisoned in darkness his whole life. Other guest roles followed, including an appearance on *Restless Gun*, and then came his movie break in the cult classic *I Was a Teenage Werewolf*. In 1959, he got the lead in another "B" film *The Legend of Tom Dooley*. During the film's

second week of production, Eli Orowitz had a fatal heart attack near the movie theater he managed; he had just finished carrying film reels up five flights of stairs. Deeply grieved over his father's death, Landon later called the filming of *Tom Dooley* a disaster.

Little Joe Cartwright

But the film wasn't a complete disaster, because it brought Landon to David Dortort's attention. After seeing the film, he became Dortort's only choice for Little Joe Cartwright. Weighing only 132 pounds when *Bonanza* began, Landon wore sweatshirts under his costume to add bulk. He earned $500 a week for his role, a far cry from the $20,000+ each week he earned later on but a fine salary for 1959. He later described cashing his first *Bonanza* paycheck and ordering egg roll after egg roll in a cheap Chinese restaurant in Hollywood. "The waiter thought I was out of my mind," he said. "They probably still talk in that restaurant about the wide-eyed kid who ate one egg roll after another."

But Michael Landon wasn't happy just acting. He remembered nice guys like his father inevitably failing, and tried to gain creative control over every aspect of his career. One Friday in 1962 the actors were told they didn't have a new script and they should take the next week off. Landon couldn't afford to. By then he was making alimony payments to Dodie and had married his second wife, Lynn Noe. Lynn had a daughter and the new family needed money. Landon wrote "The Gamble" over the weekend, and the episode aired on April 1, 1962. In this episode the Cartwrights stop in the town of Alkali after a profitable cattle drive with $30,000 in their saddlebags. The sheriff and his henchmen rob exactly $30,000 from the bank, kill a clerk and frame the Cartwrights. Little Joe escapes from jail and it's up to him to free his family. He later called the script, "not as good as some scripts, better than some scripts, a lot better than not working."

But even writing wasn't enough. Landon directed his first *Bonanza* episode in 1971, after a

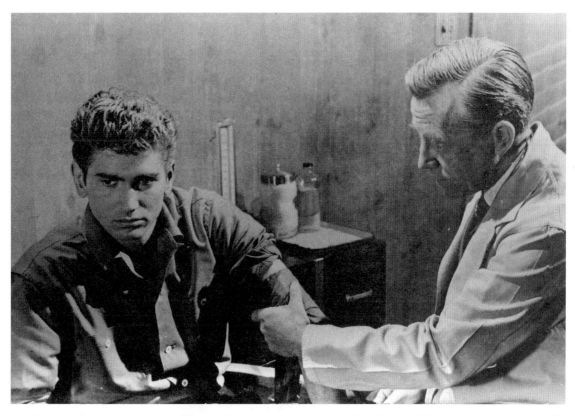

Mad scientist Tony Marshall and James Dean wanna-be Michael Landon in "I Was A Teenage Werewolf"

press conference in which one of the reporters asked if any of the actors would ever direct any episodes. "Sure they will," Dortort replied, probably not meaning it. Michael Landon jumped at the chance, asking, "when?" When Dortort said, "soon", Landon asked, "soon, when?" Dortort had no choice but to allow Landon to direct and write "To Die In Darkness", a favorite among fans even today.

One of Landon's best writing and directing jobs was "Kingdom of Fear", (April 4, 1971). The Cartwrights and Candy are arrested for trespassing. Everyone in their prison camp is there for the same crime, and no one has ever escaped. The camp's owner has discovered the cheapest possible labor for his mine — slave labor. The tension level is among the highest in *Bonanza*'s run, an amazing feat for the end of the eleventh season, when it's easy to sink into a formula.

Landon's demand for creative control brought disagreements with NBC. They protested portions of his scripts, which Landon called "a lot

of bull." "You begin to get the feeling that somebody's just trying to think of something to write down so they can send a memorandum," he told reporters. He heard through the grapevine that some people thought he didn't write the scripts — he wasn't capable. "It's not that they were surprised that I wrote the scripts," he said. "They were surprised I could write my own name." Despite his gray hair, many still thought of him as Little Joe. "Sometimes they even let me ride into Virginia City by myself," he said.

One of Landon's trademarks was short scripts. "People don't talk that much or that easily," he said. The best example of his quiet scripts is the fourteenth season opener "Forever". Landon had meant the script as a showcase for his close friend Dan Blocker. Hoss was to marry, but joy turns to tragedy in the second half of the two-hour show when Hoss' pregnant wife is brutally murdered. When Dan Blocker died suddenly on May 13, 1972, Joe was featured as the tragic groom. Although Landon suspected the audience

Michael Landon wasn't just a pretty face; he constantly fought for creative control. Here, he directs Lorne Greene and guest star James Whitmore in "To Die in Darkness", his directorial debut.

might want an entire memorial episode for the gentle giant, he refused to do one, adding only three lines about Hoss' death. "That's all that needs to be said," he explained. "It's not necessary to discuss his death; you wouldn't do that in real life. The important things remain silent."

Landon made many public appearances and, like his co-stars, couldn't comprehend the adulation. "Did you know a guy with a department store in Pennsylvania is giving me $3,000 just to show up at a lunch this weekend?" he told Look magazine in 1964. Like Lorne Greene and Dan Blocker, he was booked nearly every day not spent filming. In 1964, he logged over 250,000 air miles doing everything from opening automobile dealer showrooms ($7,500) to headlining telethons ($3,000). His 15-minute act consisted mostly of

lame humor about Dan Blocker. "My brother Hoss loves to dance," he said. "You should see that boy do the twist. He looks like a runaway truck and trailer." Landon's critics tried to criticize the teen idol for having a "spoiled Hollywood image." He dissapointed them at each stop by visiting the local hospital. "It may sound hokey," he said. "but when a parent writes and says his child is very sick, if I can spend half an hour in the room, that's 30 of the happiest minutes of the child's life. Not because is me, Mike Landon the actor. They don't even know what I look like. What they see is what they expect — Little Joe Cartwright from the Ponderosa."

Landon shared a business manager with Lorne Greene and Dan Blocker and invested his *Bonanza* fortune wisely both on his own and with his two co-stars. By 28 the shaggy-haired actor was an unlikely-looking business executive — he was vice-president of a seat-belt manufacturing firm, one-third owner of a potato-packing plant, and a principal shareholder in a modernistic condominium development overlooking the Pacific. In 1964, while Little Joe was asking, "Pa, can I borrow the horse tonight?" Michael Landon entered a 15-acre land deal with Greene and Blocker to the tune of $400,000.

Landon was known for a terrific sense of humor, both on and off-screen. The three actors frequently horsed around between scenes. Shortly after Blocker's death, Landon confessed lunchtimes on the set were hardest for him — that's where thirteen years of pranks came to mind. On-screen, his comedic scenes with Dan Blocker were often as funny as Laurel and Hardy. There's a long list of classics to pick from: "Joe Cartwright-Detective", where Joe applies Scotland Yard techniques to Virginia City; "Ponderosa Explosion", where Joe and Hoss breed rabbits for fur coats and are overrun with adorable little animals they don't have the heart to skin; "Old Sheba", where Joe and Hoss receive a elephant as payment for circus work, and many more.

Landon didn't consider retiring after *Bonanza*'s run, although the show had made him a multi-millionaire. He developed *Little House on the Prairie* after considering dozens of ideas. *Little House* went on for ten seasons, and Landon controlled the show throughout as its executive producer. Most of his crew had worked with him on *Bonanza*, and continued with him on *Highway to Heaven* and *Us*, the series he was planning when he died.

Landon's marriage to Lynn Noe ended bitterly in 1981. Their relationship seemed idyllic to everyone, including their children, for most of its nineteen years. But Landon had starting dating Cindy Clerico, a makeup artist on *Little House* and a stand-in for Melissa Sue Anderson. Lynn discovered the affair, and the divorce settlements dragged on for over a year. Michael married Cindy in 1983.

Michael Landon had grown from an unhappy child to one of the most accomplished entertainers in the world. He had devoted his career to depicting the ideal family he never had. But no story was more compelling than his last: his battle with pancreatic cancer in 1991. He approached it with his trademark strength and humor.

When the tabloids had taken one-too-many cheap shots at him and his family, Landon appeared on *The Tonight Show* to confront the rumors. Of course, he had gotten requests from every talk show in America, but Johnny Carson had been his friend for years. It turned out to be the second-highest rated *Tonight Show* of all time.

The appearance was not at all morbid; Carson and Landon discussed some of their favorite practical jokes. They discussed a recent dinner at a Malibu restaurant. As they left, Johnny backed his car over the owner's cat. The cat screeched and took off. The owner told them not to worry; he would take care of the cat. Later, Landon told Johnny the cat had died, but then laughed and admitted the cat was fine. When they went back to the restaurant, Michael substituted fake menus, featuring such dishes as Kitten Carson, Pussy Mousse a la Mercedes, and Tureen of Tabby.

That show was his last public appearance. Landon died in his Malibu home on July 1, 1991, leaving behind his wife, Cindy, nine children, several grandchildren, various animals and 25 years of beloved television footage. A fine legacy.

Film and Television Credits

Stories of the Century, "Shadows of Belle Starr"
  (SYN, 1956)
Adventures of Jim Bowie, "Deputy Sheriff" (ABC, 9/28/56)
Adventures of Jim Bowie, "The Swordsman"
  (ABC, 12/14/56)
Wire Service, "High Adventure" (ABC, 12/20/56)

Frontier Doctor, "Belle Starr" (SYN, 1957)
DuPont Theater, "The Man from St. Paul" (ABC, 1/29/57)
Telephone Time, "Fight for the Title" (CBS, 3/17/57)
G.E. Theater, "Too Good with a Gun" (CBS, 3/24/57)

Schlitz Playhouse of the Stars, "The Restless Gun"
(CBS, 3/29/57)
Tales of Wells Fargo, "Shotgun Message" (NBC, 6/10/57)
Court of Last Resort, "The Forbes-Carol Case"
(NBC, 10/18/57)
Matinee Theater, "The Weak and the Strong"
(NBC, 10/29/57)
Tales of Wells Fargo, "The Kid" (NBC, 11/18/57)

U.S. Marshal, "The Champ" (SYN, 1958)
Trackdown, "The Pueblo Kid" (CBS, 4/4/58)
Schlitz Playhouse of the Stars, "Way of the West"
(CBS, 6/6/58)
Alcoa Theater, "Johnny Risk" (NBC, 6/16/58)
Student One, "Man Under Glass" (CBS, 7/14/58)
Wanted: Dead or Alive, "The Martin Poster"
(CBS, 9/6/58)
Tombstone Territory, "The Rose of Rio Bravo"
(ABC, 9/17/58)

The Rifleman, "End of a Young Gun"
(ABC, 10/14/58)
The Texan, "The Hemp Tree" (CBS, 11/17/58)
Trackdown, "Day of Vengeance" (CBS, 11/28/58)

Wanted: Dead or Alive, "The Legend" (CBS, 3/7/59)
Tombstone Territory, "The Man From Brewster"
(ABC, 4/24/59)
Playhouse 90, "Project Immortality" (CBS, 6/1/59)
The Rifleman, "Mind Reader" (ABC, 6/30/59)
Johnny Staccato, "The Naked Truth" (NBC, 9/10/59)
Bonanza (series, NBC 9/12/59 to 1/16/73)

Cheyenne, "White Warrior" (ABC, 2/22/60)

Luke and the Tenderfoot (pilot episode)
(CBS, 8/6/65)

Goodyear Playhouse, "Giant Step" (NBC, 4/28/68)

Little House on the Prairie
(TV movie, NBC, 3/30/74)
Little House on the Prairie (series)
(NBC, 9/74 to 9/82)

The Loneliest Runner (TV movie, NBC, 12/20/76)
Barbara Walters Special (ABC, 5/30/78)

The Hanna Barbera Arena Show (NBC, 6/25/81)

Little House: A New Beginning, "Home Again"
(NBC, 2/7/83)
Love is Forever (TV movie, NBC, 4/3/83)

Little House: Look Back to Yesterday
(TV movie, NBC)
Little House: The Last Farewell (TV movie, NBC)

Highway to Heaven (series, NBC)

Frame tray puzzle from Artcraft, 1962

Terrifying buxom Yvonne Lime in "I Was A Teenage Werewolf"

One of David Canary's finest moments on Bonanza was the episode "To Die in Darkness", where Candy and Ben are trapped in an underground mine

David Canary: Cure for the Middle-Aged Spread

"I have a face like a bowl of oatmeal thrown against the kitchen wall," David Canary told TV Guide shortly after he joined *Bonanza*.

His reference to his squashed chin probably had millions of women flinging their oatmeal in all directions. Don't try this at home - even the most precise toss will bear little resemblance to David Canary. Eat your oatmeal, spare your kitchen walls, and catch David Canary on *Bonanza* reruns.

When Canary joined *Bonanza* in the ninth season (1967), the show was falling out of its accustomed number-one spot. After knocking out a long list of contenders, *Bonanza* met its match in the *Smothers Brothers*, a hip show more in tune with the late 60's. Tom Smothers said "*Bonanza* is suffering from middle aged spread."

So David Dortort created Candy, a young, free-spirit who's not afraid to strike first and ask questions later. Candy is much more independent than Hoss and Joe, relieving what insiders called "da-da-ism." "Candy is a loner, a stray," Dortort explained. "He is not a Cartwright so he is not necessarily bound by family ties. He has no Ben Cartwright to fall back upon in solving his problems."

Canary, who was 29 years old at the time, was the natural choice to play Mr. Canaday (no first name was given, adding to the character's mystery). Canary was born and raised in

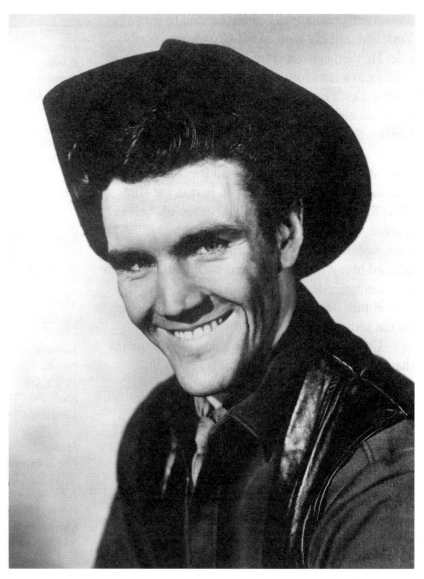

Massillon, Ohio, the son of a J.C. Penney store manager. His wanted to sing, but it was impossible to avoid football in Massillon, so he forgot about his baritone voice in favor of the town pastime. "Football was not a sport where I came from," he told TV Guide. "Winning was everything to a point of insanity...I broke my nose in the Indiana game my sophomore year at Cincinnati. Not just broke it — I shattered the whole thing.

We won 21-0." He was one of the smallest men (5-11½) ever to be drafted onto the Denver Broncos. He turned them down in favor of acting.

After graduation, Canary headed to New York and quickly won an off-Broadway chorus role. He then appeared frequently in bit parts, leading to a lead role in off-Broadway's "The Fantasticks". He entered the army in 1962, and there directed a military production of "The Fantasticks" and acted in nine other shows. His big break came in 1964 when he rejoined "The Fantasticks" in San Francisco and was spotted by Universal Studios. That led to a part in the film "The Saint Valentine's Day Massacre" as well as television appearances on *Peyton Place*, *Gunsmoke* and *Cimarron Strip*. David Dortort noticed him when he appeared with Paul Newman in "Hombre", describing him as "the kind of kid who comes on and suddenly there's nobody else on the screen."

Canary got the kind of welcome on *Bonanza* that every new kid dreams of. There was no resentment from the show's cast and crew, and everyone felt that he added a great deal to the show. "We're all so damn goody-goody, we can't get involved anymore," Dan Blocker told TV Guide. "The kid is great. The show needs him."

Canary appeared regularly on *Bonanza* from 1967-1970, made one appearance in 1971, and returned in the 14th and last season. In between he had tried unsuccessfully to write and direct his own films. The list of must-see Candy episodes is too long to list. Consult the episode guide for seasons 9-11 and 14, and don't forget "Kingdom of Fear" from season 12.

After *Bonanza*, Canary went on to achieve great success in daytime soap operas. He can now be seen on ABC's *All My Children*, in the emmy-award winning role of twin brothers Adam and Stuart Chandler. Female fans continue to swoon.

Film and Television Credits

Peyton Place (series) (ABC, 1/65)

Gunsmoke, "Nitro" (CBS, 4/8, 4/15/67)
Gunsmoke, "Tiger by the Tail" (CBS, 1967)
Bonanza (series) (NBC, 1967-1971 and 1973)
Dundee and the Culhane, "The Dead Man's Brief" (CBS, 10/4/67)
Hombre (1967)
The St. Valentine's Day Massacre (1967)

Cimarron Strip, "Knife in the Darkness" (CBS, 1/25/68)

The FBI, "The Last Job" (ABC, 9/26/71)
Hawaii Five-O, "3000 Crooked Miles to Honolulu" (CBS, 10/5/71)
Bearcats, "Hostages" (CBS, 10/14/71)
Alias Smith and Jones, "Everything Else You Can Steal" (ABC, 12/16/71)

Alias Smith and Jones, "The Strange Fate of Conrad Meyer Zulick" (ABC, 12/2/72)

Incident on a Dark Street (TV movie) (NBC, 1/13/73)
The Rookies, "Down Home Boy" (ABC, 11/19/73)
Police Story, "Death on Credit" (NBC, 11/27/73)
Kung Fu, "Theodora" (ABC, 1973)
Kung Fu, "The Elixir" (ABC, 12/20/73)

Melvin Purvis - G-Man (TV movie) (ABC, 4/19/74)
The Rookies, "A Test of Courage" (ABC, 12/2/74)

Johnny Firecloud (1975)
Posse (1975)
Shark's Treasure (1975)
S.W.A.T., "Kill S.W.A.T." (ABC, 9/20/75)

The Dain Curse (miniseries) (CBS, 5/22, 5/23, 5/24/75)

Another World (series) (NBC, 1981 to 1983)

American Playhouse, "King of America" (PBS, 1/19/82)

All My Children (ABC, 1983 to present)

David Canary clowning on the set of "All My Children"

A perfect target for Ben's infinite fatherly advice – Mitch Vogel as Jamie Hunter Cartwright

Mitch Vogel: The Fourth Cartwright Son

"Can you believe that I was still in my playpen when *Bonanza* started?" Mitch Vogel told TV Guide in 1971. "The show is older than my five pigeons, my rabbit and my chameleon combined."

Mitch Vogel joined *Bonanza* in 1970 when he was 13 years old. By 1970 Michael Landon was 34 and Dan Blocker had passed the big 4-0. Ben's fatherly advice, no matter how well Lorne Greene delivered it, began to sound silly. The father-son bond was key to *Bonanza*'s success and without it the show was on shaky ground. "We got the feeling that the warmth of the show was in danger of being weakened by the absence of the father-son relationship," Dortort explained. Mitch Vogel as Jamie Hunter (later Jamie Cartwright) added much-needed youth to *Bonanza*, and became a perfect victim of Ben's fatherly advice.

A native of Alhambra, California, Vogel lived with his mother, half-sister and grandmother. His grandmother also doubled as his business manager. While his *Bonanza* co-stars were signing multi-million dollar land deals, Vogel's grandmother allowed him $3.00 a week. "It isn't too bad," he said. "I get lunch money too."

Vogel fell in love with acting in 1966 when his mother took him to see *Peter Pan*. He enrolled in the Orange County Performing Arts Foundation, which led to lead parts in community productions of *Tom Sawyer*, *Heidi* and *The Wizard of Oz*. His performances caught the attention of an agent. Vogel appeared in "Yours, Mine and Ours" with Henry Fonda and Lucille Ball, "The Reivers" with Steve McQueen, and "Menace on the Mountain" and "Bayou Boy", both for the Wonderful World of Disney. In "Bayou Boy", he filmed a scene with an alligator. Vogel was in the lake when the alligator opened its mouth, and Vogel stared down the throat of the giant reptile - the wires on his jaw had snapped. Vogel shoved an oar into the alligator's mouth and made tracks!

The youngest *Bonanza* cast member by far, Vogel earned his co-stars' respect. "It takes a pretty bright kid to change hats as he does and handle the script with such ease," Lorne Greene said. To test Vogel's abilities, during a rehearsal Greene ad-libbed lines and movements. Another kid might have been shaken up, but Vogel kept up.

Filming *Bonanza* around Vogel's schedule was a new challenge for the cast and crew. According to law a child Vogel's age can work just 4 hours each day and must receive 3 hours of tutoring. To manage that tight schedule, Vogel showed up at 8am sharp and went from makeup and wardrobe to private tutoring. He was also tutored between scenes. This difficult schedule was worth the effort; Vogel added a great deal to the show. In an era of political and social unrest, it was great to hear Ben's advice sounding as fresh as it had many years earlier.

Film & Television Credits

The Virginian, "The Storm Gate" (NBC, 1968)

Gunsmoke, "McCabe" (CBS, 1970)
Bonanza (series, NBC 1970-1973)

Gunsmoke, "Lynch Town" (CBS, 1973)

The Streets of San Francisco, "Jacob's Boy" (ABC, 1974)
Little House on the Prairie, "The Love of Johnny Johnson" (NBC, 1974)

Little House on the Prairie, "To See the World" (NBC, 1975)
Gunsmoke, "The Hiders" (CBS, 1975)

The Quest, "Seventy-Two Hours" (NBC, 1976)

Victor Sen Yung rehearses a scene with Dan Blocker

Victor Sen Yung: The Best Dag-Burn Cook In The Territory!

"You listen Hop Sing. Hop Sing 'A' number one cook. Will cook whatever you like."

Hop Sing has become an institution - even people who never watched *Bonanza* know him! For fourteen years, his scrumptious meals filled the Cartwrights' bellies while his mannerisms kept us laughing. But very little is known about Victor Sen Yung, the veteran actor who gave life to Nevada's favorite cook.

Born and raised in San Francisco's Chinatown, Sen Yung never realized a lifelong ambition to see his homeland. He majored in animal husbandry at the College of Agriculture at Berkeley with an eye toward working in China. He later switched to economics. He thought he would realize his dream during World War II, when he requested units headed for China. He missed a transfer to the 22nd Field Hospital Unit by two days, and instead was assigned to the Air Force's "Winged Victory" unit. Finally, when he heard a China-bound unit was being organized, he applied and was sent to Berkeley's Chinese Language School to learn Mandarin (he spoke fluent Cantonese). He received his orders to go to China, but the war ended before he was shipped out.

Yung began acting in 1938 when, while working for a chemical company, he brought some samples to 20th Century Fox to sell them a new flame-proofing substance. They didn't buy it, but they did test him for Charlie Chan's "Number Two Son". "There was nothing to it," he said later. "A cocky American kid. I was like that anyway." He appeared in 11 Chan movies with Sidney Toller for 20th Century Fox, and another 14 for Monogram. He appeared in over 300 movie and television roles, playing bankers, doctors, bartenders and spies. He was billed as Sen Yung early in his career, and added Victor in the early 1940's.

Victor Sen Yung never actually cooked anything on *Bonanza*. If the menu called for bacon and eggs, a prop man cooked it. Anything more complicated, like a barbecued side of beef, was ordered from an outside caterer. Sen Yung was an accomplished Cantonese cook, but the Cartwrights never ordered egg foo yung.

He was paid very little for his work on *Bonanza*. "I haven't gotten wealthy off anything," he told TV Guide, "except in experience and friends." To supplement his income, he worked for a public relations firm marketing Chinese food. "I read the fortunes, but I don't eat the cookies," he said.

It's sadly ironic that Victor Sen Yung was killed by a stove. He died alone and penniless in his tenement apartment on November 9, 1980, of a gas leak . He was 65 years old.

Film and Television Credits

Charlie Chan in Honolulu (1938)

Charlie Chan at Treasure Island (1939)
Charlie Chan in Reno (1939)

Charlie Chan at the Wax Museum (1940)
Charlie Chan in Panama (1940)
Charlie Chan's Murder Cruise (1940)
The Letter (1940)
Murder Over New York (1940)

Charlie Chan in Rio (1941)
Dead Men Tell (1941)

Across the Pacific (1942)
Castle in the Desert (1942)
The Mad Martindales (1942)
Moontide (1942)
Night Plane from Chungking (1942)

China (1943)

Dangerous Millions (1946)
Dangerous Money (1946)
Shadows Over Chinatown (1946)

The Chinese Ring (1947)
The Trap (1947)

Docks of New Orleans (1948)
The Feathered Serpent (1948)
The Golden Eye (1948)
The Shanghai Chest (1948)

Chinatown After Midnight (1949)
Oh, You Beautiful Doll (1949)

The Breaking Point (1950)
A Ticket to Tomahawk (1950)

The Groom Wore Spurs (1951)
Valley of Fire (1951)

Target Hong Kong (1952)

Forbidden (1953)

Trader Tom of the China Seas (1954)

Blood Alley (1955)
The Left Hand of God (1955)

Bachelor Father (Series) (1957-62)
Men in War (1957)

The Hunters (1958)
She Demons (1958)

Bonanza (Series) (1959-73)
The Saga of Hemp Brown (1959)

Flower Drum Song (1961)

Confessions of an Opium Eater (1962)

Kung Fu (1972) (TV)

The Red Pony (1973) (TV)

The Man with Bogart's Face (1980)

A wonderful early caricature of our heroes

Hey Pa, what's a bus doing in the background of our publicity photo?

Hoss sports his new wristwatch, though it wasn't invented for another forty years.

Two great memorabilia pieces:
Top: Michigan Rummy game
Right: Ponderosa Party Time LP

"Four-color" comic from Dell. The four-colors preceded comic #1, and were released to test the market.

The Cartwrights shelter a pair of young elopers and are caught in a web of Spanish vengeance!

Bonanza #1

Another four-color

VICTORIA

TV WEEK

MAY 27, 1967   10c

JOHNNY YOUNG BOMBSHELL!

MICHAEL LANDON
Bonanza

Next three pages: TV Weeks/TV Times from Australia

TV WEEK

VICTORIA

1/-

SEPTEMBER 1, 1962

MICHAEL LANDON
and LORNE GREENE
of Bonanza

TV TIMES

10¢

FEBRUARY 14, 1960

Dan Blocker,
Lorne Greene and
Michael Landon of
BONANZA

Season 1

1. A Rose for Lotta, *September 12, 1959*

Ben won't sell mining tycoon Alpheus Troy Ponderosa timber to support his operations. Troy hires Lotta Crabtree to lure a Cartwright into her room so Troy can hold him for ransom. When Lotta's wagon "breaks down" on the Ponderosa, Joe falls for the beauty and escorts her to her hotel.

Guest Stars: Yvonne DeCarlo, George Macready

Written by: David Dortort

Directed by: Edward Ludwig

2. The Sun Mountain Herd *(alternate title: Death on Sun Mountain), September 19, 1959*

Mark Burdette and Early Thorne plan to kill the Indian antelope and sell the meat to miners. They do well until Ben finds Chief Winnemuca on the Ponderosa stealing cattle. He offers meat to the miners at a lower price than Burdette and Thorne, and the two retaliate by disguising as Indians and attacking miners en route to the Ponderosa.

Guest Stars: Barry Sullivan, Leo Gordon

3. The Newcomers, *September 26, 1959*

Blake McCall crosses the Ponderosa on his way to California. Blake's business is hydraulic mining, which destroys the land. Ben orders Blake off his land but Blake's partner, John Pennington, explains that he is bringing his sister Emily (also Blake's fiancee) to a better climate to cure her respiratory disease. Ben asks Hoss to escort them across the Ponderosa. Blake then has his men shoot an old man in the back and blames it on the Cartwrights. After Blake is defeated, Hoss falls in love with Emily, but is learns she has just a month to live. Emily is the first in a long line of women who meets an untimely end after meeting a Cartwright.

Guest Stars: Inger Stevens, John Larch

Written by: Thomas Thompson

Directed by: Christian Nyby

4. The Paiute War, *October 3, 1959*

Trader Mike Wilson mistreats two their Paiute women and attempts to escape punishment by placing the blame on Adam. A war between the Paiutes and the militia follows and the Paiutes seize Adam as a hostage. (Based on true events from May and June, 1860.)

Guest Stars: Jack Warden, Anthony Caruso, Mike Forest

Written by: Gene L. Coon

Directed by: Paul Landres

5. Enter Mark Twain, *October 10, 1959*

This episode is based on Twain's stint as a Virginia City reporter from 1862 to 1864. Twain writes a tale about a wild man living on the outskirts of the Ponderosa. The man is actually a teenage girl hiding after her father's murder. Twain prints an unacceptable retraction which angers the Cartwrights. But when Twain learns a judicial candidate is attempting to steal part of the Ponderosa, he helps the Cartwrights keep their land.

Guest Stars: Howard Duff, John Litel, Dorothy Green

Written by: Harold Shumate

Directed by: Phil Landres

6. The Julia Bulette Story, *October 17, 1959*

Joe falls in love with saloon-owner Julia Bulette, a much older woman. Ben and the town disapprove of the relationship. Julia gives money to Virginia City's development, and she treats the ill during an epidemic, yet the town is still ashamed of her. This episode is based on prostitute Julia Bulette's murder.

Guest Stars: Jane Greer, Alexander Scourby

Written by: Al C. Ward

Directed by: Christian Nyby

7. The Saga of Annie O'Toole,
October 24, 1959

Annie O'Toole and her father, Kevin "Himself" O'Toole, arrive in the gold country with two claims filed by her fiancé, Swede Lundberg. Himself dies, and when Lundberg shows up he tells Annie he sold one of his claims to Gregory Spain but can't remember which. But Annie, following her father's last wish, buried him on claim one and refuses to move him to claim two. Spain takes Annie to court. This episode is based on a true story.

Guest Stars: Ida Lupino, Alan Hale, John Patrick

Written by: Thomas Thompson

Directed by: Joseph Kane

8. The Philip Diedeshiemer Story,
October 31, 1959

Gil Fenton is superintendent of a mine recently plagued by deadly cave-ins. The mine's owner, Gil's future father-in-law Andrew Holloway, refuses to make the mine safer. Adam works with Philip Diedesheimer to improve the mine's safety. After Gil is killed in a cave-in, Diedesheimer designs a "square-set" timbering system to improve safety, but Holloway still refuses to spend the money. This episode is based on Diedesheimer work in December, 1860.

Guest Stars: John Beal, Mala Powers, Mae Marsh, R.G. Armstrong, Charles Cooper

Written by: Thomas Thompson

Directed by: Joseph Kane

"Help me, boys – my finger's glued to the map, and it's about to catch fire."

9. Mr. Henry T.P. Comstock,
November 7, 1959

This episode is based on the discovery of the Comstock Lode and the founding of Virginia City in 1859. Henry Comstock secures part of a silver fortune. When two miners announce a gold strike, Comstock says he owns the land they were prospecting. Meanwhile, Joe courts Sarah, the daughter of Chief Winnemuca. Between the Chief's disapproval and the miners' fight over the strike, Virginia City is in turmoil.

Guest Star: Jack Carson

Written by: David Dortort

Directed by: John Brahm

10. The Magnificent Adah,
November 14, 1959

Ben's old friend, actress Adah Issacs Mencken, is in Virginia City touring in the play Mazeppa. Her former love, drunken has-been John Regan, is following her. Ben moves into a room at her hotel to protect her. His sons, convinced their father is seeing a bad woman, try to prevent Adah from seeing Ben.

Guest Star: Ruth Roman

Written by: Donald S. Sanford

Directed by: Christian Nyby

11. The Truckee Strip, *November 21, 1959*

Silver baron Jason Cauter wants timber growing on disputed property between the Ponderosa and Luther Bishop, the Cartwrights' neighbor. Bishop won't sell until the dispute is settled, so Cauter refuels the feud between the Cartwrights and the Bishops. Meanwhile, in a modern telling of Romeo and Juliet, Joe and Amy Bishop plan to marry despite the feud.

Guest Stars: James Coburn, Carl Benton Reid, S. John Launer

Written by: Herman Groves

Directed by: Christian Nyby

12. The Hanging Posse, *November 28, 1959*

Three men stop at the Johnson ranch, and one kills Vannie Johnson. Her husband, Flint, forms a posse to capture the men. Adam and Joe feel Flint wants to lynch the men, so they join to prevent a lynching.

When Flint kills one fugitive who was trying to surrender, the two Cartwrights separate from the posse to find the others before Flint does.

Guest Star: Onslow Stevens

Written by: Carey Wilbur

Directed by: Christian Nyby

13. Vendetta, *December 5, 1959*

Ben is wounded during a bank holdup, but he kills a member of the Morgan gang. Carl Morgan announces that he will kill Ben. Virginia City's residents are terrified, so Hoss and a wounded Ben fight the battle assisted only by drunken Tom Prior and Doc Travis, who doesn't know how to fight.

Guest Star: Mort Mills

Written by: Robert E. Thompson

Directed by: Joseph Kane

14. The Sisters, *December 12, 1959*

Adam becomes involved with Sue Ellen Terry, a girl with a reputation. Adam is arrested after Sue Ellen is shot dead while stepping off his carriage. A lynch mob forms outside the Virginia City jail, and Adam must prove his innocence.

Guest Stars: Buddy Ebsen, Fay Spain

Written by: Carey Wilber

Directed by: Christian Nyby

15. The Last Hunt, *December 19, 1959*

While hunting deer, Hoss and Joe find a Shoshone Indian girl about to give birth. They build a shelter and Hoss delivers the baby. He sees the baby's eyes are blue, indicating a white father. Hoss and Joe are unaware the girl is seeking her white husband while her father, the Shoshone chief, is seeking her.

Guest Stars: Chana Eden, Steven Terrell

Written by: Donald S. Sanford

Directed by: Christian Nyby

16. El Toro Grande, *January 2, 1960*

Ben sends Hoss and Joe to Monterey with $15,000 to purchase a prized Spanish breeding bull named "El Rojo Grande" (The Big Red). While there, Joe falls for Cayetena Losaro whose father, Don Xavier Losaro, owns the bull. Cayetena's fiance, Eduardo Montalban, fights with Joe. The fight is interrupted when El Rojo Grande disappears; Don Xavier's young son loves the bull, and does not want him sold.

Guest Stars: Barbara Luna, Ricardo Cortez

Written by: John Tucker Battle

Directed by: Christian Nyby

17. The Outcast, *January 9, 1960*

Virginia City turns against Leta Malvet after her father and brother are hanged for murder. She turns to convicted bank robber Clay Renton, despite the Cartwrights' warnings. Clay plans to steal the Cartwrights' payroll. When that fails, he sets his sights on a local store while the town is at the Virginia City fair.

Guest Stars: Susan Oliver, Jack Lord

Written by: Thomas Thompson

Directed by: Lewis Allen

18. House Divided, *January 16, 1960*

Fred Kyle tries to buy gold and silver for the Confederacy. He finds Virginia City equally divided in their allegiance to North or South. Joe, whose mother was from New Orleans, is easily swayed by Kyle. Joe clashes with Adam, who was born in New England.

Guest Stars: Cameron Mitchell, Stacy Harris, Mickey Simpson, Marianne Stewart

Written by: Al C. Ward

Directed by: Lewis Allen

19. The Gunmen, *January 23, 1960*

Hoss and Joe are jailed for murder in Texas. They resemble the Slade brothers, killers involved in a feud between the Hadfields and the McFaddens. (Blocker and Landon also play Big Jack Slade and Shorty Jim Slade.) Alonzo McFadden thinks they are the Slade brothers and breaks them out of jail to kill Anse Hadfield. Joe and Hoss ask the two families' women to settle the feud, which began thirty years earlier over an alleged stolen hog.

Guest Stars: Henry Hull, Ellen Corby

Written by: W. Carey Wilbur

Directed by: Christian Nyby

20. The Fear Merchants, *January 30, 1960*

Andrew Fulmer runs for Virginia City mayor on a platform of hatred for Chinese. He hires men to scare Chinese out of town. When one of Fulmer's men bothers Sally Ridley, Jimmy Chong tries to stop him. Fulmer's man tells Sally's father, J.R. Ridley, that Jimmy was causing the trouble. Ridley draws his gun and accidentally kills his daughter. Ridley blames Jimmy, and before long a lynch mob forms outside Jimmy's cell.

Guest Stars: Gene Evans, Buddy Lee, Pat Michon

Written by: Frank Unger, Thomas Thompson

Directed by: Lewis Allen

21. The Spanish Grant, *February 6, 1960*

Former dancer Rosita Morales claims to be Spanish noblewoman Isabella Marie Inez de la Cuesta, heir to a land grant which includes part of the Ponderosa. Ben doesn't want to give up any land, but agrees to obey the law. He first suspects the woman when her uncle kills a rancher who won't obey an eviction notice. Then a cowboy tells Ben Isabella is a fake. Ben sends Hoss and Joe to Monterey to investigate the grant, and he sends Adam to locate Dona Theresa Esperanza, the only one who can identify the woman in question.

Guest Stars: Patricia Medina, Sebastian Cabot

Written by: David Dortort, Leonard Heideman, Morris Lee Green

Directed by: Christian Nyby

22. Blood on the Land, *February 13, 1960*

Sheepherder Jeb Drummond fattens his sheep on the Ponderosa. The Cartwrights, fearing sheep will destroy grassland, tell Drummond to leave, but he ignores them. When Adam confronts Jeb, he kidnaps Adam. The ransom is the whole Ponderosa.

Guest Star: Everett Sloane

Written by: Robert E. Thompson

Directed by: Felix Feist

23. Desert Justice, *February 20, 1960*

The wife of Marshal Dowd is murdered, and Dowd arrests Dave Walker, one of Ben's ranch hands. The Cartwrights visit Dave and discover the Marshal has beat him. Adam and Hoss go along with Dowd to bring Dave to his Los Angeles trial. On the way they find that guilt or innocence are not obvious.

Guest Stars: *Claude Akins, Wesley Lau*

Written by: *Donald S. Sanford*

Directed by: *Lewis Allen*

24. The Stranger,
February 27, 1960

New Orleans Police Inspector Charles Leduque tries to spoil Ben's bid for the Nevada governorship. Twenty years earlier, Ben killed Simon LaRoche in self-defense and fled. Inspector Leduque was accidentally crippled by his own gun while trying to arrest Ben. He threatens to disclose the reason Ben defended himself against Simon LaRoche - LaRoche had blackmailed Joe's mother Marie who feared her past would tarnish her husband. Ben agrees to drop the campaign and surrender, unaware that charges were dropped years earlier.

Guest Star: *Lloyd Nolan*

Written by: *Leonard Heideman, Oliver Crawford*

Directed by: *Christian Nyby*

25. Escape to the Ponderosa,
March 5, 1960

After Adam is bushwhacked, the Cartwrights join an Army unit headed by Captain Bolton to track three escaped prisoners suspected of the crime. But Ben suspects the Captain after Bolton beats one of the prisoners when he won't turn in his accomplices.

Guest Stars: *Joe Maross, Grant Williams, James Parnell, Gloria Talbott, Chris Alcaide*

Written by: *Robert E. Thompson, Bill Barrett, Malcolm Stuart Boylain*

Directed by: *Charles F. Haas*

26. The Avenger, *March 19, 1960*

After Ben and Adam are convicted of murder, a young man named Lassiter takes up their cause. Lassiter's parents were lynch victims and he is determined not to let that happen to others.

Adam saves the day in "Blood on the Land"

Guest Stars: *Vic Morrow, Jean Allison*

Written by: *Clair Huffaker*

Directed by: *Christian Nyby*

27. The Last Trophy, *March 26, 1960*

The Cartwrights are visited by Ben's old friends Lord Marion and Lady Beatrice Dunsford. When Marion is attacked but won't defend himself, his wife turns away. Once a top hunter, Marion has lost his nerve. Beatrice wants a "real man" and chooses Adam. Ben helps his friend regain his bravery through a cougar hunt.

Guest Stars: *Hazel Court, Edward Ashley*

30. Feet of Clay, *April 16, 1960*

The Cartwrights take in Billy Allen after his mother dies. His father, Vance, is in prison. Billy is lonely and Hoss comforts him. Vance breaks out of jail, robs a stagecoach and kills the driver. He then comes to the Ponderosa and turns Billy against Hoss. When Hoss kills Vance in self-defense, Billy is crushed.

Guest Stars: *David Ladd, Logan Field*

Written by: *John Furia, Jr.*

Directed by: *Arthur Lubin*

28. San Francisco (a.k.a. San Francisco Holiday), *April 2, 1960*

Ben declares a San Francisco holiday after a cattle drive, and two cowhands are shanghaied for a Hong Kong bound boat. Ben looks for them but he too is kidnapped. It's up to Hoss, Joe and Hop Sing to rescue them before the ship sails.

Guest Stars: *Robert Nichols, O.Z. Whitehead*

Written by: *Thomas Thompson*

Directed by: *Arthur Lubin*

29. Bitter Water, *April 9, 1960*

Len Keith, a miner, wants to purchase land adjacent to the Ponderosa from rancher Andy McKaren. Andy's son, Tod, is anxious to sell; Keith has offered him a partnership and he is in love with Keith's daughter. When Ben tells Andy that a mine would foul the water, Andy agrees not to sell. Keith plants tick-infested cattle in a Ponderosa herd to turn Andy against the Cartwrights.

Guest Stars: *Don Dubbins, Merry Anders, Robert F. Simon*

31. Dark Star, *April 23, 1960*

Hoss and Joe find a gypsy girl named Tirza and bring her to the house. She tells Joe she is a witch born under a dark star. Tirza's group won't claim her – they too believe she is a witch. But Joe doesn't care; he has fallen in love.

Guest Stars: *Hugo Haas, Susan Harrison*

32. Death at Dawn, *April 30, 1960*

A gang sells protection to merchants and kills those who refuse to buy. One victim is store owner Cameron. Although Beth Cameron saw Farmer Perkins kill her husband, she freezes on the witness stand. Mob leader Sam Bryant bails Perkins out of jail. The Cartwrights bring Perkins back to trial, where he is sentenced to hang. Bryant kidnaps Ben and says that if Perkins hangs, so does Ben. Hoss and Joe clash with Adam, who wants to hang Perkins, certain that Bryant is bluffing. (Beth Cameron is played by Nancy Deale, who later married Lorne Greene.)

Guest Stars: *Robert Middleton*

Written by: *Laurence Mascott*

Directed by: *Charles F. Haas*

Season 2

33. Showdown, *September 10, 1960*

After Sam Kirby and his gang rob the bank, Kirby becomes a Ponderosa ranch hand while his men hide. By sticking around he can steer a posse away and keep his friends informed of developments. But his cynicism is shaken by Ben's kindness.

Guest Stars: Ben Cooper, Jack Lambert

Written by: Dean Riesner

Directed by: Lewis Allen

34. The Mission, *September 17, 1960*

Drunkard Charlie Trent feels responsible for the massacre of soldiers he had led years earlier. When Captain Pender needs a scout, Hoss suggests Charlie, who insists Hoss come along. While on the trail the soldiers find water poisoned by Cutter, Charlie's predecessor.

Guest Stars: Henry Hull, Peter Whitney, John Dehner, Harry Carey Jr.

35. Badge Without Honor,
September 24, 1960

Deputy Marshal Gerald Eskith wants to take Jason Blaine to San Francisco to testify against the Murdock gang. Adam tries to prevent Eskith, since the gang has threatened Blaine. When his plea to the judge fails, he rides along to protect Blaine.

Guest Stars: Dan Duryea, Fred Beir, Christine White

Written by: John Twist

Directed by: Arthur Lubin

36. The Mill, *October 1, 1960*

Tom Edwards incorrectly feels Ben caused the accident that crippled him. In this loose version of Othello, Tom drinks with his evil ranch hand Ezekiel. Ben and his sons build a mill on the Edwards ranch to help Tom feel productive. But Ezekiel tells Tom that his wife is having an affair with Adam.

Guest Stars: Claude Akins, Harry Townes, Dianne Foster

Written by: Halsted Wells

Directed by: John Rich

37. The Hopefuls, *October 8, 1960*

A Quaker wagon train headed by Jacob Darien is passing through. When two drunks harass Jacob and his daughter, Regina, Adam steps in. He is attracted to Regina and escorts the wagons. Sam Bord also assists – but he plans to take the group's life savings.

Guest Stars: Larry Gates, Patricia Donahue, Dennis Patrick

Written by: E. Jack Neuman

Directed by: James Neilson

38. Denver McKee, *October 15, 1960*

Joe waits for Connie McKee to return from her Eastern school. Connie's father, Denver McKee, was a respected lawman and Indian scout, but he now leads a murderous gang. Denver never wanted any killing but his accomplices won't let him leave.

Guest Stars: Franchot Tone, Natalie Trundy

Written by: Fred Freiberger, Steve McNeil

Directed by: Jacques Tourneur

39. Day of Reckoning, *October 22, 1960*

After Matsou the Indian saves Ben's life, Ben gives him a parcel of Ponderosa land. Matsou cuts his hair and learns to farm. But Matsou's former tribe kills the wife of Ike Daggett, Ben's neighbor who hated Indians. Ike Daggett kills Matsou's pregnant wife as revenge, which drives Matsou to torture Ben, who he blames for transforming him.

Guest Star: Ricardo Montalban

Written by: R. Hamer Norris, Leonard Heideman

Directed by: Richard Bartlett

40. The Abduction, *October 29, 1960*

Hoss and Joe take their dates to the carnival. Carnival owner Phil Reed likes Jennifer Beale, Joe's date, and imprisons her. No one except Reed's girl-friend will help; when she is killed Joe is arrested.

Guest Stars: Gerald Mohr, Jackie Russell

Written by: Herman Groves

Directed by: Charles F. Haas

41. Breed of Violence, *November 5, 1960*

Sheriff Kincaid is strict with his daughter, Joe's friend Dolly. To escape his tyranny she leaves town with Vince Dagen, unaware that he has robbed a bank. She learns the truth when he and his companions kill a guide while trying to kidnap the Cartwrights.

Guest Stars: John Ericson, Myrna Fahey, Val Avery

Written by: David Lang

Directed by: Johnny Florea

42. The Last Viking, *November 12, 1960*

Ben's brother-in-law, Hoss' uncle Gunnar Borgstrom, is headed to Canada for a raid with his gang. While at the Ponderosa his men take Joe and his girlfriend Carrie hostage.

Guest Stars: Neville Brand, Sonja Wilde, Al Ruscio

43. The Trail Gang, *November 26, 1960*

Outlaw Johnny Logan joins a Ponderosa cattle drive under the name Sam Jackson. He seeks revenge on the sheriff who imprisoned him a year earlier, and the drive will pass through that sheriff's town. The sheriff is Johnny's father.

Guest Stars: Dick Davalos, James Westerfield, Edgar Buchanan, Robert J. Wilke

44. The Savage, *December 3, 1960*

Adam discovers a white woman with the Shoshone Indians. The Indians believe the White Buffalo Woman has magical healing powers, but they realize she is mortal when one of them touches her. Adam rescues her when they try to kill her, but he is hit by an arrow. While the woman, Ruth Halversen, nurses him, he learns she was raised by the Bannock Indians.

Guest Stars: Anna-Lisa, Hal Jon Norman

45. Silent Thunder, *December 10, 1960*

Joe becomes friends with a deaf-mute named Ann Croft and teaches her sign language. Ann's father feels the two are too close. Ann loves Joe, but Joe thinks of her as a friend. Meanwhile, a ranch hand loves Ann and would do anything to get her, even kill her father.

Guest Stars: Stella Stevens, Albert Salmi, James Griffith, Kenneth MacKenna, Sherwood Price

Written by: John Furia, Jr.

Directed by: Robert Altman

46. The Ape, *December 17, 1960*

Hoss becomes friends with Arnie Gurne, a huge retarded man. Arnie loves Shari the saloon girl, but when she spurns him he accidentally kills her.

Guest Stars: Leonard Nimoy, Cal Bolder

47. The Blood Line, *December 31, 1960*

Luke Grayson is killed by Ben in self-defense. His teenage son Todd comes from back East to avenge his father's death. He didn't know his father was a criminal. Ben feels guilty and responsible for Todd.

Guest Stars: Lee Van Cleef, Jan Sterling, David Macklin

48. The Courtship, *January 7, 1961*

Ben's friend Josh Layton has drunk himself to death, and Ben sends Hoss and Joe to Sacramento to see his widow, Helen. Hoss is shocked to see she's young and beautiful. He suggests she return to the Ponderosa. They become engaged on the way. Adam returns from San Francisco, where he's learned that Helen is a gambler and is probably only using Hoss.

Guest Star: Julie Adams

Written by: Richard N. Morgan

Directed by: James P. Yarbrough

49. The Spitfire,
January 14, 1961

Joe must shoot Jeb Hoad when he catches him setting fire to some timber and unsuccessfully orders him to stop. Jeb's daughter Willow tells Joe the Hoads will kill the Cartwrights. Grandma Hoad and her boys come to the Ponderosa. Their first target is Adam, who they shoot in the leg.

Guest Stars: Katherine Warren, Jack Elam

Written by: Ward Hawkins

Directed by: William Dario Faralla

50. The Bride,
January 21, 1961

While Ben's away, Jennifer Lane comes to town claiming to be his wife. When he returns she realizes the man she married in Crater Plains was an impostor. Ben and Hoss take her to Crater Plains, and Ben is arrested for the murder of Ned Birch, an old miner. Suddenly, Jennifer turns on Ben and backs up the charge.

Guest Stars: John McIntire, Suzanne Lloyd, Adam West

Written by: Richard Newman

Directed by: Alvin Ganzer

51. Bank Run, *January 28, 1961*

When Joe overhears banker Harrison planning to claim insolvency, close the bank and steal the funds, he and Hoss decide to "rob" the bank. But Ben, Adam, and all of Virginia City are unaware of their motives, and the two find themselves on wanted posters. A very funny episode.

Guest Stars: Walter Burke, Ian Wolfe

Written by: N.B. Stone, Jr.

Directed by: Robert Altman

52. The Fugitive, *February 4, 1961*

When retired Ponderosa foreman Will Reagan hears of his son Carl's death, he asks Adam to go down to

Our Land, Our Heritage – an excellent, and extremely rare album. Fortunately, it is on the Bear Family CD box set.

Plata, Mexico, to investigate. Adam learns Carl was jailed for murder and was killed while trying to escape. Adam gets no help from the sheriff, and is beaten by two men. He finally uncovers the truth: Carl is not dead.

Guest Star: Frank Silvera

Written by: Richard Landau

Directed by: Lewis Allen

53. Vengeance, *February 11, 1961*

Willie Twilight has been drinking and brawling, and when Hoss comes to the aid of Willie's girlfriend, Mary, he accidentally kills Willie. Hoss feels terrible about the death. After Willie's brother Red shoots Hoss in the back, Doc Martin tells Ben that Hoss has lost the will to live.

Guest Stars: Adam Williams, Beverly Tyler

Written by: Marion Parsonnet

Directed by: Dick Moder

54. Tax Collector, *February 18, 1961*

Good for nothing Jock Henry becomes the local tax collector. He assesses residents for outrageous amounts, earning a two percent commission. He neglects his pregnant wife and mare, Ellen and Sally, respectively. With the townspeople, wife, and mare miserable, the Cartwrights devise a scheme to make Jock quit his job. When two species go into labor simultaneously, Hoss has his hands full.

Guest Stars: Eddie Firestone, Kathie Browne

Written by: Arnold Belgard

Directed by: William Witney

55. The Rescue, *February 25, 1961*

After Ben loses a fistfight with Josh Tatum, the boys feel he may be getting old and should take it easier. Rustlers have been stealing cattle and the boys convince him to stay home while they investigate. Hoss gets shot in the leg, and all three run out of food and water, so Ben must rescue his sons.

Guest Stars: Leif Erickson, Richard Coogan

Written by: Steve McNeil

56. The Dark Gate, *March 4, 1961*

Adam's friend, Ross Marquett, is suddenly acting peculiar. He beats his wife Delphine after accusing her of having an affair with Adam. He then robs a gold shipment with a group of outlaws. Adam fears Ross is suffering from insanity.

Guest Stars: James Coburn, CeCe Whitney

Written by: Ward Hawkins

Directed by: Robert Gordon

57. The Duke, *March 11, 1961*

An English prizefighter who fancies himself a champion with his fists and with women comes to town seeking a ring opponent. His first challenger is Hoss, who vows to teach him a lesson.

Guest Stars: Maxwell Reed, Randy Stuart, J. Pat O'Malley, Jason Evers

Written by: William R. Cox, Theodore and Mathilde Ferro

Directed by: Robert Altman

58. Cut Throat Junction, *March 18, 1961*

The Sierra Freight Line has frequently been robbed. Ben, his sons, and Sierra troubleshooter Ted Trask find the stolen merchandise, but Trask is wounded. While recovering, he gets a wire terminating him after ten loyal years. He decides to join the outlaws.

Guest Stars: Robert Lansing, Shirley Ballard

Written by: Nat Tanchuck

Directed by: Dick Mader

59. The Gift, *April 1, 1961*

Joe buys his father a white Arabian stallion for his birthday. While returning with the stallion and a vaquero named Emeliano, he comes into an Indian uprising led by Cochise. Trapped in the desert with food and water running out, they seek help. A group of Comancheros led by Sam Wolfe are willing to help in exchange for the horse.

Guest Stars: Martin Landau, Jim Davis

Written by: Denne Petticlerc, Thomas Thompson

Directed by: William Witney

60. The Rival, *April 15, 1961*

Hoss has a friendly rivalry with Jim Appelgate for the affections of Cameo Johnson. He sees his rival riding away from a lynching, but if he turns Jim in Cameo will think he's only trying to get rid of his rival. So Hoss must solve the mystery of the vigilantes.

Guest Stars: Peggy Ann Garner, Charles Aidman

Written by: Anthony Lawrence

Directed by: Robert Altman

61. The Infernal Machine, *April 22, 1961*

Hoss and his friend Daniel Pettibone ask Virginia City residents to finance Pettibone's horseless carriage. The two are ridiculed until Throckmorton comes to town and invests $1,000 in the project. He also convinces many others to invest and runs off with the money. Sheriff Roy must arrest Pettibone before Virginia City lynches him.

Guest Stars: George Kennedy, Eddie Ryder

Written by: Ward Hawkins

Directed by: William Witney

Joseph, where's your costume?

62. Thunderhead Swindle, *April 29, 1961*

Unemployed miners have been stealing Ponderosa cattle for food. Ben learns of a strike at the Thunderhead Mine. Knowing the mine is all played out, he talks to former owner Jim Bronson. They suspect the new owners, Jack Cunningham and Frank Furnas, have been salting the mine to swindle investors. Then Bronson is murdered.

Guest Stars: Parley Baer, Vito Scotti

Written by: Gene L. Coon

63. The Secret, *May 6, 1961*

Joe is arrested for the murder of Mary Parson. Joe didn't see her that night, but his friend John Hardner says he saw them together. Mary's family says she was planning to elope with Joe. Then the doctor tells Deputy Connelly that Mary was pregnant.

Guest Stars: Russell Collins, Morgan Woodward

Written by: John Hawkins

Directed by: Robert Altman

64. The Dream Riders, *May 20, 1961*

Ben's old friend Major John Cayley comes from the East to conduct a hot air balloon experiment for the Army. With him are his daughter, Diana, and two soldiers. But in reality the men are AWOL, and they're planning to rob the bank and escape in the balloon.

Guest Stars: Sidney Blackmer, Burt Douglas

Written by: Jack McClain, James Van Wagoner

Directed by: Robert Altman

65. Elizabeth, My Love, *May 27, 1961*

Ben recalls the time he served as first mate on Captain Abel Morgan Stoddard's ship. He married the captain's daughter Elizabeth. Shortly after Ben and Elizabeth were married the captain was forcibly retired. He couldn't live without the sea and considered running a slave ship. Worry over her father weakened Elizabeth, who was pregnant with Adam. She died in childbirth, and Ben took his infant west.

Guest Stars: Geraldine Brooks, Torin Thatcher

Written by: Anthony Lawrence

Directed by: Lewis Allen

66. Sam Hill, *June 3, 1961*

Traveling blacksmith Sam Hill, known for his extraordinary strength and toughness, has one soft spot; he refuses to sell the land where his mother is buried. When his long lost father, John Henry Hill, sells it to Colonel Tyson, Sam vows to die first.

Guest Stars: Claude Akins, Ford Rainey

Written by: David Dortort

Directed by: Robert Altman

Season 3

67. The Smiler, *September 24, 1961*

Hoss fights with drunk Arthur Bolling when he insults the Widow McClure. Bolling is killed when his own gun goes off. The widow's testimony exonerates Hoss. After the funeral, a guitar-strummin' stranger comes to town. He is Arthur's brother Clarence. He says he forgives Hoss for his brother's death, but beneath the surface he plans revenge.

Guest Stars: Hershel Bernardi, Scatman Crothers

Written by: Lewis Reed

Directed by: Thomas Carr

68. Springtime, *October 1, 1961*

In a hilarious mud wrestle with his brothers, Joe accidentally hits Jebediah, an old friend of Ben's, with a piece of wood. Jebediah pretends to be injured and Ben asks him to give the boys tasks as compensation. Adam must evict a delinquent couple. Hoss must buy a couple out of their home. And Joe must throw a squatter off Jebediah's land.

Guest Stars: John Carradine, John Qualen

Written by: John Furia, Jr.

Directed by: Christian Nyby

69. The Honor of Cochise, *October 8, 1961*

Captain Moss Johnson has killed some of Chief Cochise's braves. He arrives at the Ponderosa pursued by warriors. Ben is disgusted, but won't turn him over. Ben convinces Cochise to let him go to Fort Churchill to bring back the commanding officer, Colonel Clinton Wilcox. But Wilcox won't accompany Ben.

Guest Stars: Jeff Morrow, DeForest Kelley

Written by: Elliott Arnold

Directed by: Don McDougall

70. The Lonely House, *October 15, 1961*

During Joe's visit to widow Lee Bolden, a wounded man stumbles in. Joe recognizes him as Trock, and Joe knows he got his wound while robbing the bank. Lee removes the bullet and falls in love with Trock. To tell Lee the truth would break her heart and kill the wounded man.

Guest Stars: Paul Richards, Faith Domergue

Written by: Frank Chase

Directed by: William Witney

71. The Burma Rarity, *October 22, 1961*

Henry Morgan and Phil Axe sell a $50,000 emerald to Clementine Hawkins for $25,000. They then switch it with a glass imitation. Joe and Hoss steal the fake and pursue the crooks. But Clementine was on to the scam and had switched the gems back! She agrees to drop theft charges against the boys if Ben marries her.

Guest Stars: Beatrice Kay, Wally Brown

72. Broken Ballad, *October 29, 1961*

Adam befriends former gunfighter Ed Payson, just returned from prison. General store owner Will Cass doesn't want Payson back. Payson had killed Cass' son in a gunfight.

Guest Star: Robert Culp

Written by: John T. Kelley

Directed by: Robert Butler

73. The Many Faces of Gideon Flinch, *November 5, 1961*

Gideon Flinch and his niece hide from Bullethead Burke, who claims Gideon's advice lost him $5,000. Burke and Flinch had never met, so Flinch's niece asks Hoss to pose as him to protect her uncle. But Joe likes the niece, pays a boy to tell Hoss the Ponderosa is on fire, and pretends to be Flinch to capture the girl's attention. But he doesn't know what's in store.

Guest Stars: Ian Wolfe, Arnold Stang, Sue Anne Langdon

Written by: Robert Vincent Wright

Directed by: Robert Altman

74. The Friendship, *November 12, 1961*

Prisoner Danny Kidd saves Joe's life. At Joe's request Ben wins a parole, but he gives Joe responsibility for Danny. Danny has difficulty adjusting to freedom, but Joe promises to stay with him, no matter how much he objects.

Guest Stars: Dean Jones, Janet Lake

75. The Countess, *November 19, 1961*

Widow Lady Linda Chadwick visits Ben. Twenty years earlier she had declined his marriage proposal. Ben's employees have heard rumors that he is broke and insist on being paid cash daily. Ben learns the rumor was started by Chadwick's secretary Montague to force him to marry Chadwick for her money.

Guest Stars: Margaret Hayes, John Anderson

Written by: William R. Cox, William D. Powell

Directed by: Robert Sparr

76. The Horse Breaker, *November 26, 1961*

The Cartwrights' horse breaker, Johnny Lightly, is paralyzed. Doctor Kaye sends his assistant, Ann Davis, to the Ponderosa to help with therapy. He flirts with Ann, but she's cold; she had been hurt before. Johnny attempts suicide. But when Nathan Clay, who hates Ben, threatens to burn down the Ponderosa, Johnny pulls himself out of his depression and pulls Ann out of hers.

Guest Stars: Ben Cooper, R.G. Armstrong

Written by: Frank Chase

Directed by: Don McDougall

77. Day of the Dragon, *December 3, 1961*

Su-Ling, a Chinese slave owned by General Tsung, is kidnapped by Gordon and Barrett. They lose her to Joe in a poker game. Joe brings her home to ask Pa's advice, and he says to free her, but she won't leave. She likes her new master. General Tsung tracks her down and is willing to kill to get her back.

Guest Stars: Lisa Lu, Richard Loo, Philip Ahn, Mort Mills

Written by: John T. Dugan

Directed by: Don McDougall

78. The Frenchman, *December 10, 1961*

A stranger claims to be reincarnated 15th century poet Francois Villon. He and his sister Eloise visit the Ponderosa. The Cartwrights are taken with Eloise but not Francois, especially after he steals a horse, buggy and some valuables. He has decided he must be hung as his namesake was four centuries earlier.

Guest Stars: Andre Phillips, Erika Peters

Written by: Norman Lessing

Directed by: Christian Nyby

79. The Tin Badge, *December 17, 1961*

In the small town of Rubicon, mine owner Ab Brock and Mayor Goshen plan a murder. They want an inexperienced sheriff, and when Joe passes through town they set him up to win a fight against the town bully. By the time he realizes something's funny, he won't let himself quit.

Guest Stars: Vic Morrow, Karen Steele

Written by: Don Ingalls

Directed by: Lewis Allen

80. Gabrielle, *December 24, 1961*

The Cartwrights find blind orphan Gabrielle Wickham wandering through the snow. She's seeking her grandfather Zacariah, the hermit of Davidson Mountain. Zachariah spent twenty years in jail for a crime he didn't commit and now wants nothing to do with anyone. The Cartwrights throw a lavish Christmas party to cheer up the girl.

Guest Stars: Diane Mountford, John Abbott

Written by: Anthony Lawrence

Directed by: Thomas Carr

81. Land Grab, *December 31, 1961*

Settlers buy Ponderosa land from Bragg, an ex-army officer and old friend of Ben's. When Ben tries to evict them, he is shown legal-looking documents signed "John Polk." By the time Ben discovers "Polk" is really Bragg, two settlers are dead.

Guest Stars: John McGiver, George Mitchell

Written by: Ward Hawkins

Directed by: Orrick McDearmon

82. The Tall Stranger,
January 7, 1962

Hoss loves the banker's daughter, Margie Owens, but before he proposes Mark Conners wins her hand with tales of foreign adventure. Hoss later finds her in a Carson City hospital giving birth. She dies and Conners returns from wandering to get his daughter, who he thinks he can sell to his father-in-law.

Guest Stars: Sean McClory, Kathie Browne

Written by: Ward Hawkins

Directed by: Don McDougall

83. The Lady From Baltimore, *January 14, 1962*

Deborah Banning wants her daughter, Melinda, to marry Joe. Deborah married Horace, a loser, and wants her daughter to do better. Melinda doesn't love Joe but obeys her mother. Ben shows Deborah that money isn't as important as love.

Guest Star: Mercedes McCambridge

Written by: Elliott Arnold

Directed by: John Peyser

84. The Ride, *January 21, 1962*

A disguised man robs the Goat Springs stage line and kills Toby Barker. Adam is certain the killer is his friend Bill Enders. Witnesses said they saw Bill in Virginia City ninety minutes after the killing and insist it's impossible to ride from Goat Springs to Virginia City in that time. Adam must prove them wrong.

Guest Stars: Jan Merlin, Grace Gaynor

Written by: Ward Hawkins

Directed by: Don McDougall

85. The Storm, *January 28, 1962*

Ben gets a visit from old friend Captain Matthew White and his daughter Laura. Laura surprises all when she announces her plans to marry childhood sweetheart Joe. To his surprise, Joe falls in love with her all over again.

Lorne Greene's "The Man", available on the Bear Family CD box set

Guest Stars: Brooke Hayward, Frank Overton

Written by: Denne Petticlerc

Directed by: Lewis Allen

86. The Auld Sod, *February 4, 1962*

Danny Lynch wrote his mother in Ireland a blarney about the huge ranch he owns. When she visits, the Cartwrights pose as ranch hands so Danny can tell her the Ponderosa is his.

Guest Stars: Cheerio Meredith, James Dunn

Written by: Charles Lang

Directed by: William Witney

87. Gift of Water, *February 11, 1962*

During a drought farmers begin moving to the grasslands. Ben's neighbors fear overgrazing and threaten to kill anyone who enters. Ben and his sons work with one farmer to get water from underground.

Guest Stars: Royal Dano, Pam Smith, James Doohan, Majel Barrett

Written by: Borden Chase

Directed by: Jesse Hibbs

88. The Jackknife, *February 18, 1962*

The Cartwrights are plagued by rustlers. While scouting, Adam finds injured Matthew Grant. He brings him home and finds he has a wife and son. Adam cleans up the unkempt ranch and suspects Grant is a rustler. He hopes Grant will give himself up and face a light sentence before Ben springs his trap.

Guest Stars: John Archer, Bethel Leslie

Written by: Frank Chase

Directed by: William Witney

89. The Guilty, *February 25, 1962*

Ten years earlier, Jack Groat killed Lem Partridge's wife and was jailed. Lem now hates violence and never taught his son Jimmy to use a gun. After his release Groat provokes and shoots Jimmy as Ben looks on. He claims self-defense. Lem blames Ben, although there was nothing he could have done.

Guest Stars: Lyle Bettger, Charles Maxwell

Written by: Clifford Irving

Directed by: Lewis Allen

90. The Wooing of Abigail Jones, *March 4, 1962*

Ranch hand Hank Myers loves schoolmarm Abigail Jones, but she only likes refined men. In this funny takeoff on Cyrano DeBergerac, Hoss and Joe convince Adam to sing from the shadows while Hank mouths the words. But Abigail discovers the trick and proposes to Adam, to his dismay. Vaughn Monroe sings "Racing with the Moon."

Guest Stars: Eileen Ryan, Vaughn Monroe

Written by: Norman Lessing

Directed by: Christian Nyby

91. The Lawmaker, *March 11, 1962*

Quiet Asa Moran becomes sheriff when Roy Coffee is injured. Power corrupts him and he starts a reign of terror. He and Adam were childhood rivals. Asa knocks Adam unconscious and jails him. Ben must go up against a lawman to save his son's life.

Guest Stars: Arthur Franz, Les Tremayne

Written by: John A. Johns, Dick Nelson

Directed by: Christian Nyby

92. Look to the Stars, *March 18, 1962*

This episode is based on the life of Jewish-American scientist Albert Abraham Michelson, Nobel-Prize winner for measuring light waves. The Cartwrights help young Albert, who has been expelled by Mr. Norton, a bigoted and jealous teacher.

Guest Stars: Douglas Lambert, William Schallert

Written by: Robert M. Fresco, Paul Rink

Directed by: Don McDougall

93. The Gamble, *April 1, 1962*

The Cartwrights visit the town of Alkali after a cattle drive with $30,000. The sheriff and his henchmen rob exactly $30,000 from the bank, kill a clerk and frame the Cartwrights. Joe escapes from jail and it's up to him to free his family.

Guest Stars: Charles McGraw, Ben Johnson

Written by: Michael Landon, Frank Chase

Directed by: William Witney

94. The Crucible, *April 8, 1962*

Adam is left to die in the desert after two thieves steal $5,000 and his horse. He stumbles upon a prospector named Kane who offers to lend him a mule and supplies in exchange for three day's work. Kane turns out to be a madman who holds Adam prisoner and tortures him to prove that anyone can be driven to kill, even a man as rational as Adam.

Guest Star: Lee Marvin

Written by: John T. Dugan

Directed by: Paul Nickell

95. Inger, My Love, *April 15, 1962*

When Hoss is late for his own birthday party, Ben recalls Hoss's mother, Inger. The two met in Illinois as he and young Adam were headed west. Adam fell sick and Ben needed work to care for him. Ben defeated local bully Gunnar Borgstrom and impressed tavern owner McWhorter, who gave him a job. He fell in love with Inger Borgstrom. The two obstacles are her brother, Gunnar, and her fiancee, McWhortor.

Guest Stars: Inga Swenson, James Philbrook

Written by: Frank Cleaver, David Dortort, Anthony Lawrence

Directed by: Lewis Allen

96. Blessed Are They, *April 22, 1962*

Ben is asked to bring two warring families, the Mahans and the Clarkes, to a truce when their feud threatens to have all of Virginia City choosing sides.

Guest Stars: Robert Brown, Ford Rainey

Written by: Borden Chase, Frank Cleaver

Directed by: Don McDougall

97. The Dowry, *April 29, 1962*

Bandits steal a chest holding the dowry for Alexander Dubois' daughter. But it had phony jewels; Dubois is poor but wanted his daughter to marry landowner Ricardo Fernandez. But Fernandez too was lying about his wealth and conspiring with the thieves.

Guest Star: Steven Geray

Written by: Robert Vincent Wright

Directed by: Christian Nyby

98. The Long Night, *May 6, 1962*

Adam is ambushed by escaped convict Poindexter, who leaves Adam in prison garb. Adam catches up with and kills Poindexter in self-defense. Immediately after he's caught by a posse led by Poindexter's partner, Trace, disguised as a lawman. Trace knows Adam has a $10,000 bank draft, and threatens to let the posse lynch him unless he hands it over.

Guest Stars: James Coburn, Bing Russell

Written by: George Stackalee, E.M. Parsons

Directed by: William Witney

99. The Mountain Girl, *May 13, 1962*

Joe promises Trudy Harker's dying grandfather that he will find

Trudy's long-lost wealthy kin in San Francisco. When they agree to meet Trudy, Joe must turn the mountain girl into a lady. Trudy becomes so involved with her new family that she's ready to abandon her old life, including her fiancé Paul.

Guest Stars: Nina Shipman, Warren Oates

Written by: John Furia, Jr.

Directed by: Don McDougall

100. The Miracle Worker, *May 20, 1962*

Susan Blanchard is paralyzed in a buggy accident. A traveling healer named Garth promises to make her walk. He falls in love with Susan and tells her if she marries him she will be cured. Hoss learns Garth is a phony, but Garth insists he can prove his love for Susan by healing her.

Guest Stars: Ed Nelson, Patricia Breslin, Mort Mills

Milton Bradley puzzle #2 "To The Rescue", 1964

Big Dan Blocker SR Footballer Blocking For U. S.

WITH U. S. 45TH DIV.—Sometime during a four hour period one Sunday afternoon, a few men in the 45th Division became combat veterans instead of just soldiers.

Only a few days after the former Oklahoma National Guard division had traded brick barracks in Hokkaido, Japan, for frontline bunkers in Korea, a patrol learned plenty about the bitter irony of battle.

In a do or die fire fight with the enemy which raged for four hours, the patrol saw two of its members die and two more wounded.

The patrol, led by 1st Lt. Frank L. Garrison, Lawton, Okla., and **Sgt. DAN D. BLOCKER,** O'Donnell, Tex., ran into a Communist ambush deep in no man's land. The men elected to fight it out when a member of their patrol was wounded. His buddies were pinned down and couldn't reach him.

They weathered enemy small arms, machinegun and mortar fire, for four hours, meanwhile giving the enemy a taste of Thunderbird lead. Irony ended the action when the injured man they were fighting to reach died.

IT'S A FAR CRY from long and dusty marching at Louisiana's Camp Polk to a study of Shakespeare and Pvt. Dan Blocker of O'Donnel, Texas, soaks his weary feet as he reads. Private Blocker isn't delving into Marchette Chute's "Shakespeare of London" as a hobby. The 6-foot 4-inch Texan is slated for the leading role in "Macbeth," which will be staged at the camp by the 45th Infantry Division. Blocker studied drama for four years and has appeared in New Engand theatres. Another Texan, Pvt. Joe Pereira of Houston will be costume designer.

SERVES IN KOREA—From a forward position in Korea, two members of the 179th Regiment, 45th Infantry Division, scan enemy territory for signs of movement. The men are **Sergeant Dan Blocker** (leaning forward from foxhole), son of Mr. and Mrs. Shack Blocker of O Donnell, and Sergeant First Class Roy Worley, son of Mr. and Mrs. Albert Worley of Ardmore, Okla. Blocker is a platoon sergeant. The 45th Division, former Oklahoma National Guard unit now filled with soldiers from all sections of the country, arrived in Korea last December after several months training on Hokkaido, northernmost of the Japanese islands. It was the first National Guard division to enter a combat zone since V-J Day. (U. S. Army Photo).

Season 4

101. The First Born, *September 23, 1962*

Soon after Clay Stafford is hired, he and Joe become inseparable. After shooting a man during a card game, he tells Joe that they are half brothers. Their mother Marie had been married to Ben's friend before she married Ben. Opposed to the marriage, her mother-in-law gave the baby away and told Marie it had died. Ben discovers that Clay shot and killed another man two years earlier. But Joe won't believe his brother is no good.

Guest Stars: Barry Coe, Eddie Walker

Written by: Judith and George W. George

Directed by: Don McDougall

102. The Quest, *September 30, 1962*

Joe, tired of being babied, secures a contract to supply timber. Dave Donovan, who works for former contractor Will Poavey, gets a job as Joe's foreman. Donovan blows up a flume the men were using to float logs. Joe learns it's great to have a family to depend on.

Guest Star: Grant Richards, James Beck

Written by: John Joseph, Thomas Thompson

Directed by: Christian Nyby

103. The Artist, *October 7, 1962*

Ben befriends Matthew Raine, once a renowned artist but now a recluse since his blindness several years earlier. His housekeeper Ann Loring loves Raine and asks for Ben's help. Raine is improving until he gets an offer for a painting. In his frustration he starts to destroy his studio. His hand Gavin resents Raine. Gavin plans to make a killing off Raine's paintings.

Guest Stars: Virginia Grey, Dan O'Herlihy

104. A Hot Day For a Hanging, *October 14, 1962*

Hoss is arrested by Sheriff Tom Stedman of Dutchman Flats. Stedman knows Hoss is innocent of a recent theft, but he wants the notoriety of catching the "bank robber." A local wants to join the fun and identifies Hoss as the robber. A mob gathers to string up Hoss, and though Stedman is now on Hoss' side, it may be too late.

Guest Star: Denver Pyle

Written by: Preston Wood, Elliott Arnold

Directed by: William F. Claxton

105. The Deserter, *October 21, 1962*

The Cartwrights' neighbor, Bill Winters, is the son of Colonel Edward J. Dunwoody. Ten years earlier, Bill deserted when his father ordered him to massacre a Shoshone village. Now the Colonel wants his son arrested. A group of Shoshones kidnap Bill and sentence him to die for being the Colonel's son. The Colonel offers to exchange his life for Bill's.

Guest Stars: Claude Akins, Robert Sampson

Written by: Norman Lessing

Directed by: William Witney

106. The Way Station, *October 29, 1962*

Adam takes shelter in a way station run by Jesse and his granddaughter Marty. The station also hosts some stage riders and killer Luke Martin. Marty is desperate to see the world, and Luke agrees to bring her when he leaves. Adam prevents this and Marty is devastated. But the posse was closer than Luke thought, and he returns to hold everyone hostage.

Guest Stars: Robert Vaughn, Dawn Wells

Written by: Frank Cleaver

Directed by: Lewis Allen

107. The War Comes to Washoe, *November 4, 1962*

The civil war has spread to Nevada, which is poised to become a state. Confederate Judge David Terry hopes to become governor. He knows Ben will influence the statehood convention, so he sends his daughter, Morvath, to win over Joe. She does, but Adam, a New-Englander, won't allow his brother to marry a Confederate.

Guest Stars: Harry Townes, Joyce Taylor

Written by: Alvin Sapinsley

Directed by: Don McDougall

108. Knight Errant, *November 18, 1962*

Walter Prescott has ordered a mail order bride-to-be, Lotty Hawkins. Walter breaks his leg and Hoss offers to fetch the woman. He finds that Lotty is much younger than Walter. She falls in love with Hoss and runs away from Walter, who puts a price on Hoss' head. Lotty feels compelled to marry Walter.

Guest Stars: John Doucette, Judi Meredith

Written by: Joseph Hoffman

Directed by: William Claxton

109. The Beginning, *November 25, 1962*

Ben takes in Billy Horn, a white boy raised by Shoshone Indians. Milton Tanner files claim to one-third of the Ponderosa on a legal technicality. Billy has become attached to Ben, and he kills Tanner. Sheriff Coffee must arrest Ben's friend, but the confused young man escapes.

Guest Stars: Ken Lynch, Carl Reindel

110. The Deadly Ones, *December 2, 1962*

The Ponderosa is invaded by Mexican mercenaries under General Diaz. Diaz forces Ben to help him ambush a gold train. Diaz is wounded, and one of his men, Forsythe, plans to steal the gold.

Guest Star: Leo Gordon

111. Gallagher's Sons, *December 19, 1962*

Hoss finds two orphans named Will and Charlie Gallagher. They want to be on their own, but he insists on bringing them to their Aunt Chloe in Cantill. Hoss doesn't know the girls have their father's stolen loot, nor that henchmen are following them. No-one in Cantill knows Chloe, and Hoss is jailed for kidnapping. Will and Charlie head east, unaware the henchmen are on their trail.

Guest Stars: Eileen Chesis, Robert Strauss

Written by: Dick Nelson

Directed by: Christian Nyby

112. The Decision, *December 16, 1962*

Hoss punctures a lung on a cattle drive. Dr. Johns awaits hanging for a murder he claims was self-defense. Judge Franklin Grant refuses Ben's request to let Johns operate. Grant's wife died in Johns' care, but Grant withheld surgery until too late. The judge relents, and Johns saves Hoss. Then Ben wonders whether Johns is really a killer.

Guest Star: DeForest Kelley

113. The Good Samaritan, *December 23, 1962*

Wade Tyree's girl has left him, and Abigail Hinton is a widow with a young daughter. Hoss plays match-maker, and they enter a loveless marriage. Hoss does Wade's chores, but the more Hoss helps the more the marriage crumbles.

Guest Star: Jeanne Cooper

114. The Jury, *December 30, 1962*

As a juror in Jamie Wren's murder and robbery trial, Hoss alone believes there is reasonable doubt. Elmer Olsen, the victim's brother, plants a bill on Hoss that he swears was taken in the robbery. Now it seems Jamie bribed Hoss. Adam visits the only witness, Elmer Olsen.

Guest Star: Jack Betts, James Bell

115. The Colonel, *January 6, 1963*

Ben's old buddy Frank Medford is a poor traveling salesman. He lies about his work, even claiming he's working on a railroad survey for Ben. Frank courts Emily Colfax, and his pride won't let him tell her the truth.

Guest Stars: John Larkin

Written by: Preston Wood

Directed by: Lewis Allen

116. Song In The Dark, January 13, 1963

Adam's friend Danny Morgan is arrested for murdering Widow Baker. Someone reported hearing him singing at the time, and he is scratched; the widow had skin under her nails. Adam suspects self-righteous Reverend William Johnson but has no proof.

Guest Stars: Edward Andrews, Gregory Walcott

117. Elegy For A Hangman, January 20, 1963

Bob Jolley accuses Judge Harry Whitaker of unjustly hanging his father Carl. Whitaker is a longtime friend of the Cartwrights, but Bob convinces Adam. Adam risks his reputation by holding a hearing to uncover the truth.

Guest Stars: Keir Dullea, Otto Kruger

Written by: E.M. Parsons, Shirl Hendryx

Directed by: Hollingsworth Morse

118. Half A Rogue, January 27, 1963

Big Jim Leyton tries to steal Hoss' horse but passes out from a wound. Hoss discovers that Jim was shot breaking jail. According to Cal Stacy, Jim stole pelts and killed a man. Deputy Foster gives Hoss custody since no evidence is found. When a man named Carter is found dead, the deputy looks for Jim - but Jim has returned to the mountains. He and Hoss have a fistfight to settle the issue.

Guest Star: Slim Pickens

Written by: Arnold Belgard

Directed by: Don McDougall

119. The Last Haircut, February 3, 1963

Joe cares for Carlos Rodriguez's young son, Paco, after Duke Miller kills Carlos in a barber shop. Joe was knocked unconscious during the murder, so there are no witnesses and Miller and his henchman, Cal

Brennan, are acquitted. Joe and Paco journey to Juarez to find Paco's grandparents, and they catch up with Miller. Ironically, he is in a barber shop.

Guest Star: Perry Lopez

Written by: Charles Lang

Directed by: William Claxton

120. Marie, My Love, February 10, 1963

When Joe is hurt, Ben recalls his third wife, Joe's mother Marie. Jean DeMarigny was killed saving Ben's life. On his deathbed he asked Ben to contact his wife, Marie, in New Orleans. Ben found Marie, but she wouldn't forgive Jean for leaving her. Marius Angeville said Jean left because he believed Marie was unfaithful. Marius asked Ben to clear Marie's name, but Jean's mother hired duelist Eduard D'Arcy to kill Ben. After Ben cleared Marie's name, they headed west.

Guest Star: Felicia Farr

Written by: Anthony Lawrence, Anne Howard Bailey

Directed by: Lewis Allen

121. The Hayburner, *February 17, 1963*

Adam and Hoss buy a horse to enter in the Virginia City Sweepstakes. Hoss loses the horse in a card game. He and Adam beg Joe to lend them $160 to buy back the horse. Joe has been earning a fortune busting broncs at Enos Milford's ranch. Joe agrees to lend them $160, but if the horse wins he gets half the prize money and a third interest in the horse. If the horse loses Joe gets the horse and Adam's new rifle. Then Enos hires Joe as the rider of another horse. If he wins, Joe gets half the prize money.

Guest Stars: William Demarest, Ellen Corby

Written by: Alex Sharp

Directed by: William F. Claxton

122. The Actress, *February 24, 1963*

Joe falls in love with aspiring actress Julia Grant. She auditions for actor Edwin Booth, but is crushed when Booth says she lacks dramatic talent. Joe is secretly happy; maybe she'll settle down and marry him. But Booth sees Julia perform at the saloon and decides she would be perfect in his upcoming musical comedy. Joe cannot keep her from her dream.

Guest Stars: Patricia Crowley, Joey Scott

Written by: Norman Lessing

Directed by: Christian Nyby

123. A Stranger Passed This Way, *March 3, 1963*

During a robbery attempt Hoss loses his memory. An elderly Dutch couple, Klaas and Christina Vandervoort, takes him in and give him the name of their late son Hendrick. Ben worries that confronting Hoss with his past may be damaging. Christina decides to take Hoss to a Dutch community in Michigan. Ben makes them spend the night. If Hoss doesn't regain his memory, Ben will let him leave.

Guest Stars: Signe Hasso, Robert Emhardt

Written by: William Stuart

Directed by: Lewis Allen

124. The Way of Aaron, *March 10, 1963*

Adam and Rebecca Kaufmann, a Jew, are mutually attracted, but her father Aaron objects. Adam finds them camped; they couldn't make it home for Sabbath and can't travel until the following sundown. Adam is worried and sleeps nearby. Two outlaws cause trouble, and Adam must persuade Aaron to use violence for the first time.

Guest Stars: Aneta Corseaut, Ludwig Donath

Written by: Raphael T. Blau

Directed by: Murray Golden

125. A Woman Lost, *March 17, 1963*

While in San Francisco, Ben encounters old friend Rita Marlowe, who has become an alcoholic. He takes her home, and in Virginia City she recognizes Mase Sindell. He was a prizefighter but gave it up when he damaged an opponent's brain. When two promoters offer Rita money to get Mase into the ring, she tells him she'll marry him if he fights. She sees him being beaten and her harsh exterior breaks down.

Guest Stars: Ruta Lee, Don Megowan

126. Any Friend of Walter's, *March 24, 1963*

A barrage of gunfire forces Hoss into an old cabin. There he meets prospector Obie and his dog, Walter. The dog barely moves, yet Obie insists that Walter knows how to deal with the would-be robbers. But the dog loves to sleep.

Guest Star: Arthur Hunnicutt

Written by: Lois Hire

Directed by: John Florea

127. Mirror of a Man, *March 31, 1963*

Neither the Cartwrights nor ranch hand Jud Lally's wife, Amelia, know Jud used to be criminal Homer Barnes. Jud's twin Rube forces Jud to trade places so Rube can go with Joe to pick up a prized stallion; he intends to steal the animal. Their father Luke holds Jud and Amelia prisoner.

Guest Stars: Ron Hayes, Ford Rainey

128. My Brother's Keeper, *April 7, 1963*

Adam accidentally shoots Joe and grows furious with the barbaric western life. He romances Sheila Reardon, who also hates the west. Although Pernell Roberts didn't leave Bonanza for two more years, this feels like a final episode.

Guest Star: Carolyn Kearney, Brendan Dillon

Written by: Seeleg Lester

Directed by: Murray Golden

129. Five Into the Wind, *April 21, 1963*

A coach crashes miles from anywhere, killing the driver, and stranding Joe and five others. Trapper Howard Benson is murdered with Joe's knife. The other passengers want to hang Joe, but he's the only one who can lead them from the wilderness.

Guest Stars: Kathleen Crowley, Dabbs Greer

130. The Saga of Whizzer McGee, *April 28, 1963*

Whizzer McGee is a small man with a chip on his shoulder. Hoss gets Whizzer a job in the general store. Whizzer appears to be doing well, and even has a girlfriend, saloon singer Melissa. But Melissa loves a crook named Otis. Whizzer's room in the back of the store is adjacent to the bank vault.

Guest Stars: George Brenlin, Jeanne Bal

Written by: Robert Lyon Welch

Directed by: Don McDougall

131. The Thunder Man, *May 5, 1963*

Explosives expert William Poole kills Joe's girlfriend, Ann Wilson. Poole calls himself "Thunder Man". Ann father Fred has had a stroke and is found near Ann's body. Fred communicates to Joe that the killer was singing "New Orleans Woman".

Guest Stars: Simon Oakland, Evelyn Scott

Written by: Lewis Reed

Directed by: Lewis Allen

132. Rich Man, Poor Man, *May 12, 1963*

Virginia City laughs at Claude Miller until he stumbles upon a silver fortune. He gets revenge by buying mortgages and hiring Deputy Slauson. While Hoss, Joe and Claude's friend, Daisy, try to bring Claude to his senses, he's unaware that the Deputy has secured power of attorney over his fortune.

Guest Stars: J. Pat O'Malley, John Fielder

133. The Boss, *May 19, 1963*

Freight line owner Tom Slayden has driven off competition and now charges exorbitant rates. Joe hauls supplies to the Ponderosa and is shot by Tom's

Adam's disembodied head hovers above his family.

men. Ben has Tom arrested, but Tom shuts down operations, leaving residents to starve.

Guest Stars: *Carroll O'Connor, Denver Pyle*

Written by: *Leo Gordon and Paul Leslie Peil*

Directed by: *Arthur H. Nadel*

134. Little Man - Ten Feet Tall,
May 26, 1963

Italian immigrant Nick Biancci wants his son, Mario to be a concert guitarist. But when Nick doesn't stand up to two bullies, Mario decides his father is a weakling and he wants to be a rancher like his hero, Hoss.

Guest Stars: *Ross Martin, Denver Pyle*

Written by: *Eric Norden, Frank Arno*

Directed by: *Lewis Allen*

Season 5

135. She Walks In Beauty,
September 22, 1963

Sisters Emilia and Ragan Miller are opposites; Emilia is respectable, Ragan has used her beauty with men in San Francisco. Despite warnings from Adam, who has heard stories of Ragan, Hoss falls in love. Hoss cannot see the person she always will be, even when he sees her trying to seduce Adam.

Guest Stars: Gena Rowlands, Jeanne Cooper

Written by: William Stuart

Directed by: Don McDougall

136. A Passion For Justice,
September 29, 1963

Charles Dickens is furious that the town newspaper has serialized his novels without permission, and a scathing review by newspaperman Sam Walker angers him further. Dickens goes to the newspaper office to find it vandalized. Roy arrests him, and Dickens is fined $1,000. He won't pay and sits in jail. The Cartwrights know Dickens is no vandal, and set out to learn who framed him.

Guest Stars: Jonathan Harris, Victor Maddern, Frank Albertson

137. Rain From Heaven, *October 6, 1963*

Ben doesn't believe broke rainmaker Tulsa Weems can end a drought, but he offers money to tide Tulsa over. Tulsa has great pride, and he is jailed for threatening Ben with an empty gun. Tulsa's young daughter Mary Beth has typhoid fever, but her brother Jube won't let anyone care for her. Despite the danger, Hoss grabs the sick girl and locks the two of them in a bedroom to care for her.

Guest Star: John Anderson

138. Twilight Town, *October 13, 1963*

Joe is ambushed. He wanders into Martinville, an apparent ghost town. The strange people ask him to be their sheriff. Felix Mathews has terrorized them since

Sheriff Obrion died. Joe faces Mathews alone, until Corman and Masterson join him. Joe kills Mathews and collapses. He awakens to find his family and a deserted town. Ben tells him the legend of Martinville; the town is forever haunted by the ghosts of its cowardly citizens.

Guest Stars: Davey Davison, Stacy Harris

Written by: Cy Chermak

Directed by: John Florea

139. The Toy Soldier, *October 20, 1963*

Adam meets James Callan, a white artist with a Paiute wife and a passion for liquor. McDermott feeds Callan's craving for liquor, forcing Callan to sell his paintings for only whiskey and minimal food for the Paiutes. Adam offers the braves a job rounding up strays; they can keep half of what they bring in. But McDermott's men steal and re-brand the cattle.

Guest Stars: Philip Abbott, Morgan Woodward

Written by: Warren Douglas

Directed by: Tay Garnett

140. A Question of Strength,
October 27, 1963

A stagecoach carrying Hoss, Mother Veronica, and Postulate Mary Kathleen is attacked. When the thieves threaten Veronica, Mary gives them $10,000 the nuns had collected to start a hospital. Veronica calls Mary a coward and tells her she's unwelcome in the sisterhood. Mary knows she has a chance at the sisterhood if the money is recovered, and decides to face a seasoned criminal.

Guest Stars: Judy Carne, Ilka Windish, John Kellogg

Written by: Frank Cleaver

Directed by: Don McDougall

141. Calamity Over the Comstock,
November 3, 1963

Joe befriends a rude young "boy" named Cal, but discovers Cal is Calamity Jane. Ben and Adam don't want Jane at the Ponderosa; they know about her and her boyfriend, Doc Holliday. But Jane has taken a liking to Joe. Doc challenges Joe to a duel, and no one is better than Doc.

Guest Stars: Stefanie Powers, Christopher Dark

Written by: Warren Douglas

Directed by: Charles Rondeau

142. Journey Remembered,
November 10, 1963

After watching Hoss deliver a colt, Ben recalls Hoss' mother, Inger. Traveling west with Inger and Adam, Ben joined a wagon train led by Wilkes. The wagons were headed to Ash Hollow to meet another party when Indians robbed them. While Ben helped hunt them down, Inger gave birth to Hoss. By the time they reached Ash Hollow, the other party had come and gone. While there, a group of Indians attacked and Inger was killed.

Guest Stars: Inga Swenson, Gene Evans, Kevin Hagen

Written by: Anthony Lawrence

Directed by: Irving J. Moore

143. The Quality of Mercy,
November 17, 1963

Joe's friend Seth Pruitt kills his fiancee's father out of mercy after a cave-in breaks his back. When Seth asks Joe to say he died in the cave-in, Joe struggles with his conscience. He eventually wonders if it was a mercy killing at all; Seth had much to gain by murder. But an accusation would devastate Joe's childhood sweetheart, Seth's fiancee Sara.

Guest Stars: Unknown

Written by: Peter Packer

Directed by: Joseph H. Lewis

144. The Waiting Game, *December 8, 1963*

Laura Dayton is overcome with guilt when her husband is killed in an accident. She hated him, but is worried about her young daughter Peggy. Adam plays therapist, and a romance develops.

Guest Stars: Kathie Browne, Katie Sweet

Written by: Ed Adamson

Directed by: Richard C. Sarafian

145. The Legacy, *December 15, 1963*

While trailing poachers, Ben is shot and dismounted. Adam, Hoss and Joe find only his bloodied horse. Thinking that Ben was murdered, they split up and follow the trail of three ex-cons they suspect. Meanwhile, a peddler had found Ben. Ben hopes his sons will not take the law into their own hands.

Guest Stars: Robert H. Harris, James Best, Philip Pine, Percy Helton, Rory Stevens

Written by: Arthur Wilson

Directed by: Bernard E. McEveety

146. Hoss and the Leprechauns,
December 22, 1963

Hoss finds a box of gold and spots a "little feller in green." When he tells the story he becomes a laughing stock, until an Irishman tells Virginia City that, if they capture a leprechaun, he will hand over a box of gold for his freedom. Townspeople flock to the Ponderosa. After many hilarious scenes the Cartwrights learn the men are performers exploited by the Irishman. Hoss, identifying with people of abnormal size, works to get them accepted by Virginia City.

Guest Star: Sean McClory, Robert Sorrells, Clegg Hoyt, Billy Curtis, Frank Delfina, Roger Arroya, Nels Nelson

Written by: Robert V. Barron

Directed by: John Florea

147. The Prime of Life, *December 29, 1963*

Ben and old rival Barney Fuller compete for a lumber contract. Ben's employee Gabe Fletcher is killed by a piece of equipment. Ben feels guilty and retires to the house. The boys try to carry on, but Barney is luring away Ponderosa workers. It's up to Gabe's daughter Martha to help Ben.

Guest Stars: Jay C. Flippen, Melora Conway, Dan Riss, Ralph Moody

Written by: Peter Packer

Directed by: Christian Nyby

148. The Lila Conrad Story, *January 5, 1964*

Dance hall girl Lila Conrad kills Dolph Rimbeau in self-defense. She hides in the Cartwrights' supply wagon. The Cartwrights try to get her to Virginia City for a fair trial. While on the trail, they must deal with vengeful townspeople and their traveling companion, Judge Knowlton, who tries to seduce Lila.

Guest Stars: Andrew Duggan, Patricia Blair, Cathy O'Donnell, Don Haggerty, Lindsay Workman, Stuart Randall, Scott Peters, Don O'Kelly, Don Wilbanks

Written by: Preston Wood, George WaGGner

Directed by: Tay Garnett

149. Ponderosa Matador, *January 12, 1964*

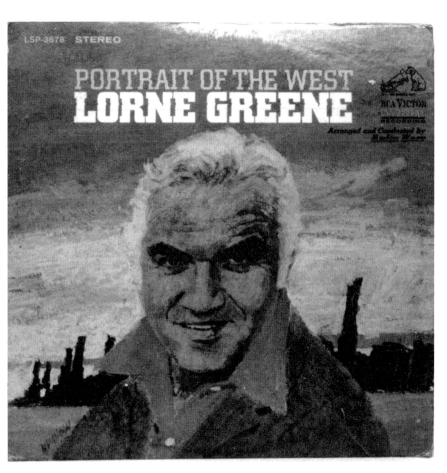

The Cartwrights are visited by Senor Tenino, and his beautiful daughter, Delores. Hoss convinces Joe that Delores loves Matadors. Joe chases overweight steers until Hoss finds him the meanest bull around, hoping that Joe will chicken out. He doesn't, and the bullfight is about to start when the bull breaks loose, creating one of the funniest scenes ever on television.

Guest Stars: Marianna Hill, Nestor Paiva

Written by: Alex Sharp

Directed by: Don McDougall

150. My Son, My Son, *January 19, 1964*

Ben has is considering marrying widow Katherine Saunders. Her son Eden was acquitted for murder three years before. Eden left town, but now he's back and vows revenge on Carl Miller, who married former girlfriend Linda. When Linda is murdered, a mob comes for Eden, who Ben protects.

Guest Stars: Teresa Wright, Dee Pollack, Sherwood Price, Zon Murray

Written by: Denne Petitclerc

Directed by: William Upton

151. Alias Joe Cartwright, *January 26, 1964*

Michael Landon plays two roles: Joe and Angus Borden, an army deserter suspected of murder. Joe is arrested. Sergeant O'Rourke believes in Joe, but Captain Merced wants him executed. We find out Merced conspired with Borden, and executing him (or appearing to) would clear his name.

Guest Stars: Keenan Wynn, Douglas Dick, Owen Bush, Hugh Sanders, Joseph Turkel, Dave Willock

Written by: Robert Vincent Wright

Directed by: Lewis Allen

152. The Gentleman From New Orleans, *February 2, 1964*

A man claiming to be Pirate Lafitte entertains the townsfolk with his tales. Ben met Lafitte during his childhood in 1812, but doesn't recognize him. The stranger helps Hoss' by collecting a debt from Amos Whittaker. Shortly after, Amos and one of his hands are killed by Lafitte's knife. Lafitte claims his knife was stolen, but Hoss alone believes him.

Guest Stars: John Dehner, Sheldon Altman

Written by: William Bruckner

Directed by: Don McDougall

153. The Cheating Game, *February 9, 1964*

This episode features Laura Dayton, who first appeared in "The Waiting Game." Here, Adam fires Laura's foreman when he neglects the ranch. Laura is furious, and declares her independence by hiring Ward Bannister. Ward claims he's a friend of Laura's late husband, and brings her his $10,000 life insurance policy. A stranger named Canfield works with Ward to sell Laura railroad stock. Ward brings Laura's daughter Peggy a wolf cub, knowing that Adam would make her free it, angering her and her mother.

Guest Stars: Kathie Browne, Peter Breck

Written by: William L. Stuart

Directed by: Joseph Sargent

154. Bullet For A Bride, *February 16, 1964*

While out hunting a mountain lion, Joe accidentally shoots and blinds Tessa Caldwell. The Cartwrights take Tessa and her family in. Before long, Joe thinks he loves her. When she regains her sight, she wants to tell Joe, but her father won't let her. He sees her marriage to Joe as a meal ticket.

Guest Stars: Marlyn Mason, Denver Pyle, Gail Bonney, John Matthews

Written by: Tom Seller

Directed by: Tay Garnett

155. King of the Mountain,
February 23, 1964

Big Jim Leyton, who we first met in the episode *Half A Rogue*, is getting married to Julie Martingale; he wants Hoss to be best man. But Jim is feuding with his future father-in-law, Grizzly, over a piece of land. Hoss suggests that a third person buy the land with Jim and Grizzly splitting the money. They choose Hoss as the impartial third party.

Guest Stars: Robert Middleton, Slim Pickens, Laurie Mitchell, Byron Foulger, Billy M. Greene, Ray Hemphill, Bruce McFarlane

Written by: Robert Sabaroff

Directed by: Don McDougall

156. Love Me Not, *March 1, 1964*

Ben and Adam make a goodwill visit to the Paiute Chief and give him a pocket watch. His gift to them is a white woman named Joan that his tribe has held captive for years. Ben tries to help her adjust to the white man's world, but Joan wants no part of it.

Guest Star: Anjanette Comer

Written by: Frank Cleaver

Directed by: Tay Garnett

157. The Pure Truth, *March 8, 1964*

Hoss' has spring fever. Ben sends him into town to be Roy's deputy, figuring he'll work off energy. Roy sends Hoss to Rimrock to pick up prisoner Earl Tusher, but Hoss goes to Red Rock, Arizona, by mistake. The Red Rock bank is robbed, and Hoss is jailed since he's a stranger in town. He breaks out and meets hermit Loulabelle Watkins Looney. She needs money to file a gold claim and decides to turn Hoss in for the reward on his head.

Guest Stars: Glenda Farrell, Lloyd Corrigan

Written by: Lois Hire

Directed by: Don McDougall

158. No Less A Man, *March 15, 1964*

Virginia City decides Sheriff Roy Coffee is too old to stand against the Wagner gang. Adam becomes his assistant, but it is Roy who captures the Wagners without bloodshed.

Guest Stars: Parley Baer, John Kellogg, Bill Zuckert, Justin Smith, Billy Corcoran, Adrienne Marden, Ed Faulkner, Ed Prentiss, Bill Clark, Joseph Breen, Rush Williams, Bob Miles

Written by: Jerry Adelman

Directed by: Don McDougall

159. Return to Honor, *March 22, 1964*

When Ben's nephew Will recovers stolen money plates, he switches identification with a corpse so the thieves will assume he died. Ben visits his nephew's grave to discover Will alive, suffering from a gunshot wound. The two return to the Ponderosa, but the thieves have caught on. After the Cartwrights defeat the outlaws in a fine fight scene, Will decides to settle down with his family.

Guest Stars: Guy Williams, Arch Johnson, Robert Wilke, Hugh Sanders, Gregg Palmer, I. Stanford Jolley, Bill Clark, James Tartan, Ralph Montgomery

Written by: Jack Turley

Directed by: Don McDougall

160. The Saga of Muley Jones, *March 29, 1964*

Whenever cousin Muley sings, he breaks glass. The Ponderosa is visited by Indian agent Thornbridge, who is about to meet with Chief White Bear when Muley sings. The Indians hear the sound of breaking glass and assume Thornbridge is firing.

Guest Stars: Bruce Yarnell, Jesse White, Strother Martin, Jerome Cowan, Bern Hoffman, Ken Drake, Ralph Moody, Billy M. Greene

Written by: Robert Barron, Alex Sharp

Directed by: John Florea

161. The Roper, *April 5, 1964*

Will Cartwright is alone in the house. Several soldiers comes by with Lee Hewitt, a wounded bank robber. Before they can continue, they're ambushed by Hewitt's men. The outlaws plan to wait until Ben returns so he can open the safe. Will realizes that Hewitt plans to kill everyone, so he pretends to side with the outlaws, opening the safe and promising to lead them to safety.

Guest Stars: Scott Marlowe, Julie Sommars

162. A Pink Cloud Comes From Old Cathay, *April 12, 1964*

Hoss orders fireworks from the Yipee Trading Company in Canton, China, but gets a wife named Tai-Lee instead. The outspoken girl encourages Hop Sing and the ranch hands to strike. A Chinese neighbor says he ordered Tai-Lee. Hoss is happy to hand her over, but she refuses. The neighbor challenges Hoss to a traditional Asian battle to win her back.

Guest Stars: Marlo Thomas, Philip Ahn, Benson Fong, William Fawcett, Mike Ragan, Phil Chambers

Written by: Lewis Clay

Directed by: Don McDougall

163. The Companeros, *April 19, 1964*

Will is visited by old friend Mateo Ibara and his wife, Carla. Ibara wants Will to return to Mexico. They fought together for Juarez, and Ibara once saved Will's life. Will feels old loyalties and plans to return, but Ben doubts Ibara's intentions.

Guest Stars: Faith Domergue, Frank Silvera, Guy Williams, Roy Engel, Rico Alaniz, Rodolfo Hoyos, Pepe Hern, Anthony Carbone

Written by: Ken Pettus

Directed by: William Claxton

164. Enter Thomas Bowers, *April 26, 1964*

Legendary opera singer Thomas Bowers has been invited to perform. But the women who invited him didn't know he was black and reject him. Roy hears of a fugitive slave and everyone assumes it is Bowers. Roy rescues him from a lynch mob led by Sam Kiley, but must arrest Bowers until he can prove his identity.

Guest Stars: William Marshall, Jason Wingreen, J. Edward McKinley, Dorothy Neumann, Robert P. Lieb, Kelly Thordsen, Alice Frost, Ken Renard, George Petrie, Ena Hartman

Written by: Leon Benson, Murray Golden

Directed by: Murray Golden

165. The Dark Past, *May 3, 1964*

Dev Farnum, a bounty hunter, is the son of a great preacher. Ben wonders why Dev has rejected God. Also staying on the Ponderosa is Holly Burnside, who is fleeing her husband Jamey Boy Briggs, the man Dev is chasing. Ben discovers Dev's dark past; during his father's services one day, his family was massacred.

Guest Stars: Dennis Hopper, Susan Seaforth, Jim Boles, Ron Starr, Lewis Charles

Written by: William Bruckner

Directed by: Murray Golden

166. The Pressure Game, *May 10, 1964*

Laura Dayton's aunt Lil decides to coax Adam to propose. She gets Laura together with Will Cartwright to make Adam jealous. The plan backfires; Laura and Will like each other. Then Laura is hurt in an accident, and Adam proposes.

Guest Stars: Kathie Browne, Joan Blondell, Guy Williams, Katie Sweet, Bern Hoffman

Written by: Don Tait

Directed by: Tay Garnett

167. Triangle, *May 17, 1964*

Laura is engaged to Adam, but she and Will can't deny their love. When Adam is paralyzed while building a house for he and Laura, she can't leave him. But while confined to a wheelchair Adam realizes it's better if Laura married Will. He struggles to his feet and Laura and Will ride off together. This is the final appearance of the dreadful Laura Dayton. Hallelujah.

Guest Stars: Kathie Browne, Guy Williams, Katie Sweet, Grandon Rhodes

Written by: Frank Cleaver

Directed by: Tay Garnett

168. Walter and the Outlaws, *May 17, 1964*

This is the second appearance of Hoss' friend Obie and his dog Walter. Obie leaves Walter with Hoss when he goes to visit his sister. Walter takes Adam's room for its southern exposure. Then he takes Joe's quilt. Then Hoss soothes Walter with a tuba. Walter disappears, and Obie returns with a ransom note. The three bumbling outlaws, Macie, Willard and Teague, have struck again.

Guest Stars: Arthur Hunnicutt, Steve Brodi, James Luisi, Vic Werber

Written by: Lois Hire

Directed by: Ralph E. Black

Season 6

169. Invention of a Gunfighter,
September 20, 1964

Joe's friend Johnny Chapman never learned to shoot. But after Al Mooney humiliates him, Johnny decides it's time to learn. Joe agrees to teach him, and the two enjoy shooting at targets. But Johnny goes too far, becoming a bounty hunter and alienating everyone, including his fiancee.

Guest Stars: Guy Stockwell, Valerie Allen, Ron Foster, Bern Hoffman

Written by: Dan Ullman

Directed by: John Florea

170. The Hostage, *September 27, 1964*

Ben is kidnapped for a $100,000 ransom. While his sons scramble to get the money, Ben tells each criminal that his partner is planning to steal the ransom.

Guest Stars: Harold J. Stone, Conlan Carter, Jacqueline Scott, Buck Taylor, Cal Bartlett, Bill Clark

Written by: Donn Mullally

Directed by: Don McDougall

171. The Wild One, *October 4, 1964*

Hoss wants to cross-breed wild stallions with Ponderosa mares. He contacts Lafe Jessup, who shoots wild horses in the leg and then beats them to break them in. Hoss fights with Lafe. Lafe had deserted his wife Prudence, a devout Quaker. He had proposed to her while sick, and now regrets it. Prudence is expecting their child. This episode was supposed to end with her dying in childbirth, but NBC ordered it changed.

Guest Stars: Aldo Ray, Kathryn Hays

Written by: Joe Pagano

Directed by: William Witney

172. Thanks For Everything, Friend,
October 11, 1964

Adam is saved from drowning by handsome drifter Tom Wilson. When he pursues Adam's friend Sue, her awkward fiancé Jerry becomes furious. When Sue's father is murdered, Jerry sees the perfect opportunity to get rid of Tom.

Guest Stars: Rory Calhoun, Linda Foster, Tom Skerritt, John Mitchum

Written by: Jerry Adelman

Directed by: Christian Nyby

173. Logan's Treasure, *October 18, 1964*

Sam Logan is out of prison. 20 years ago, he and Jack Crawford stole $100,000 in gold dust. Logan insists Crawford was lynched before he could reveal where the gold was buried. But a bounty hunter named Frank Reed doesn't believe it. When Jack's son Mike appears, Jack begins to recall where the gold is hidden.

Guest Stars: Dan Duryea, John Kellogg, Virginia Gregg, Jack Carol, Tim McIntire, Russ Bender

Written by: Ken Pettus, Robert Sabaroff

Directed by: Don McDougall

174. The Scapegoat, *October 25, 1964*

Hoss prevents Waldo Watson's suicide. He identifies with Waldo because of his huge size. Waldo is a former professional boxer fleeing his promoters. When he refused to throw a fight, they thought he accepted a bribe. Now they want the money, but he has none.

Guest Stars: George Kennedy, Richard Devon, Sandra Warner, Jon Lormer, Troy Melton, Bill Catching

Written by: Rod Peterson

Directed by: Christian Nyby

175. A Dime's Worth of Glory,
November 1, 1964

Dime store novelist Tobias Finch wants to write "The Saga of the Courageous Cartwrights" after seeing Ben and Adam defeat two stage robbers, but the men aren't interested. Finch finds Sheriff Reed Laramore cooperative; he jails the Cartwrights to get a good story without their interference.

Guest Stars: Walter Brooke, Bruce Cabot, Charles Maxwell, James Bell, Dal Jenkins

Written by: Richard and Esther Shapiro

Directed by: William Claxton

176. Square Deal Sam, *November 8, 1964*

All the Cartwrights and Hop Sing get fleeced by charming old man Sam. They all buy deeds for the same land.

Guest Stars: Ernest Truex, Sandy Kenyon, Nydia Westman

Written by: Jessica Benson, Murray Golden

Directed by: Murray Golden

177. Between Heaven and Earth, *November 15, 1964*

Joe becomes obsessed with his fear of heights when he can't retrieve a rifle from a cliff. Each night he wakes his family with screaming nightmares. Ben tells Joe that a fear doesn't make him less of a man, but it doesn't help. Ben must coax Joe up the cliff.

Joe must conquer his fear of heights in "Between Heaven and Earth"

Guest Stars: Richard Jaeckel, Bob Biheller, Bill Moss

Written by: Ed Adamson

Directed by: William Witney

178. Old Sheba, *November 22, 1964*

Hoss injures wrestler Bearcat from Tweedy's traveling circus. Hoss agrees to substitute, and Joe goes along. Tweedy soon owes them $400, but gives them an elephant named Sheba instead. Ben is furious. Hoss and Joe trade the elephant for an old mule just before Ben decides he needs Sheba to move railroad ties. Poor Hoss must carry the ties.

Guest Stars: William Demarest, Clegg Hoyt, Henry Kulky, Phil Chambers

Written by: Alex Sharp

Directed by: John Florea

179. A Man to Admire, *December 6, 1964*

Hoss' is accused of murdering Flint Durfee. He hires drunk lawyer Whitney Parker. The Cartwrights work to keep Parker sober, but with "the hanging prosecutor" from Carson City against him, Hoss' chances look slim. His only hope is the new pocket billiards table in the Silver Dollar Saloon.

Guest Stars: James Gregory, Michel Petit, Booth Colman, Dave Willock, Hal Baylor, William Mims, Jason Johnson, Jonathan Hole, Burn Hoffman

Written by: Mort R. Lewis

Directed by: John Florea

180. The Underdog, *December 13, 1964*

Ben hires half-Comanche Harry Starr. Lee Burton and his pals beat Harry. But Harry, Lee, and the others are horse thieves. Burton shows Joe a branding iron hidden in Harry's cabin. Joe finds Harry's "dead" body hanging by a noose. The outlaws staged Harry's hanging to collect the reward.

Guest Stars: Charles Bronson, Tom Reese, Bill Clark

Written by: Donn Mullally

Directed by: William F. Claxton

181. A Knight to Remember,
December 20, 1964

Adam is returning to town when his stage is robbed. But the outlaws are chased away by a knight. Adam is left holding the strongbox and is arrested. He doesn't tell the story to the local sheriff, instead asking him to wire Roy Coffee for a reference. Adam is released, but the same scene happens again, and now he tells the sheriff about the knight. The sheriff wires Ben, telling him his son has been "seeing things."

Guest Stars: Henry Jones, Robert Sorrells

Written by: Robert V. Barron

Directed by: Vincent McEveety

182. The Saga of Squaw Charlie,
December 27, 1964

Squaw Charlie is taunted by the townspeople, who want "that savage" out of town. His two friends are Ben and a young girl named Angela. Angela's mother is furious that her daughter is friends with Charlie. Two men hide the girl and convince her mother and a lynch mob that Charlie murdered her.

Guest Stars: Anthony Caruso, Virginia Christine, Don Barry, Vickie Coe, Myron Healey, William Tannen

Written by: Warren Douglas

Directed by: William Witney

183. The Flapjack Contest,
January 3, 1965

Joe throws something at Hoss and breaks a window. Ben sends Joe to town to buy a new one, but in town he learns about the $500 flapjack eating contest. Joe bets a fortune on Hoss, and must keep him on a starvation diet until the event. His other task is getting the window; each time he buys a new one, it breaks.

Guest Stars: Johnny Seven, Joan Huntington, Mel Bergen, Howard Wendell, Bern Hoffman, Olan Soule

Written by: Frank Cleaver

Directed by: William Claxton

Ben comes to Joe's rescue in "Between Heaven and Earth"

184. The Far, Far Better Thing,
January 10, 1965

When Ben is visited by old friend Martin Meldine and his daughter, Lucy, Joe and his friend Tuck compete for Lucy. But Lucy's only love is books, and the only romance she knows is Dickens' *A Tale of Two Cities*. Ben takes her to Indian's Grief, a Paiute landmark. When Paiutes attack, Lucy learns the difference between romanticism and reality.

Guest Stars: Brenda Scott, X Brands, Stacy Harris, Warren Vanders, Jack Bighead

Written by: Mort R. Lewis

Directed by: Bernard McEveety

185. Woman of Fire, *January 17, 1965*

Ben's friend Don Miguel visits with his two daughters, Margarita and Elena, and Elena's two suitors. They're on their way to meet Margarita's suitor, Don Luis. Margarita scares men away with her temper, but as the older daughter she must marry first. Adam spanks Margarita, and Don Miguel and Elena's suitors ask him to tame her. Adam is too successful. Don Luis comes to see the woman of fire he's heard about.

Guest Stars: Joan Hackett, Jay Novello, Cesare Danova, Susan Silo, Valentin De Vargas, Eugene Iglesias

Written by: Suzanne Clauser

Directed by: William Claxton

186. The Ballerina, *January 24, 1965*

Kellie Conrad dances while her father fiddles. Hoss accidentally injures Mr. Conrad's fiddling arm and takes them in until he recovers. Former ballet star Paul Mandel teaches Kellie ballet. She falls in love with Paul and with ballet, but what about her father? Frank Chase wrote the script for his sister, professional ballet dancer Barrie.

Guest Stars: *Barrie Chase, Warren Stevens, Douglas Fowley, Hugh Sanders, Read Morgan*

Written by: Frank Chase

Directed by: Don McDougall

187. The Flannel-Mouth Gun, *January 31, 1965*

The Cattlemen's Association meets to discuss the rustling problem. Ben and Adam oppose hiring a professional gunman, but are out-voted and Clegg Simmons comes to town. When the small ranchers are bought out at ten cents on the dollar, and the wife of one is murdered, Adam must learn who Clegg is working for.

Guest Stars: Earl Holliman, Robert Wilke, Don Collier, Harry Carey

Written by: Leo Gordon, Paul Leslie Peil

Directed by: Don McDougall

188. Ponderosa Birdman, *February 7, 1965*

Professor Phineas T. Klump knows one day he'll soar over the mountains. He designs a pair of feathered wings. But an injury forces Klump to watch someone else fly – his friend Hoss.

Guest Stars: Ed Wynn, Marlyn Mason

Written by: Blair Robertson

Directed by: Herbert L. Strack

189. The Search, *February 14, 1965*

Adam's double Tom Burns is spending Adam's money; Adam investigates in Placerville. Ann is a saloon girl in love with Tom, an ex-con wanted for murder. She knows Tom has been framed by partner Jason Evers. Adam and Ann search for Tom, but they find him dead, confirming Ann's suspicions.

Guest Stars: Lola Albright, Kelly Thordsen, Howard Wright, Phil Chambers, Lindsay Workman, Laura Devon, Jack Herring

Written by: Frank Cleaver

Directed by: William Claxton

190. The Deadliest Game, *February 21, 1965*

Virginia City is visited by aerial acrobats. Aging Borelli can't relinquish stardom to Carlo Alfieri. Borelli is jealous of Carlo's youth and is in love with Carlo's girlfriend, Petina, who has her eye on Joe.

Guest Stars: Cesar Romero, Ilze Taurins

191. Once a Doctor, *February 28, 1965*

Hoss and Professor Poppy, a medicine man selling cheap liquor, share "medicine." Another Englishman, Thomas Crippen, is looking for Dr. P.A. Mundy. Crippen's wife died on Mundy's operating table. Crippen finds Mundy disguised as Poppy. He breaks into Mundy's wagon, but accidentally shoots Hoss.

Guest Stars: Michael Rennie, Ashley Cowen, Elizabeth Rogers, Bill Clark, Grandon Rhodes

Written by: Martha Wilkerson

Directed by: Tay Garnett

192. Right is the Fourth R, *March 7, 1965*

Adam substitutes for injured schoolteacher Barbara. He tries to interview Colonel Scott and his friend for a territorial history course but finds them unwilling. During the founding of the Nevada territory Colonel Scott and his friend massacred Indians and stole their land; now they will do anything to cover it up.

Guest Stars: Mariette Hartley, Everett Sloane

Written by: Jerry Adelman

Directed by: Virgil W. Vogel

193. Hound Dog, *March 21, 1965*

The Cartwrights get another visit from cousin Muley Jones. He gives his feisty hounds to Hoss. But the dogs howl all night unless sung to, so sing Hoss must. The dogs' original owner Tracey appears. Her grandfather, Abner, had sold Muley the dogs because the dogs were keeping her from cooking.

Guest Stars: Bruce Yarnell, Sue Anne Langdon

Written by: Alex Sharp

Directed by: Ralph E. Black

194. The Trap, *March 28, 1965*

Joe's former girlfriend Hallie Shannon thinks Joe murdered her husband Burk so she'd marry him. Burk's twin brother Booth comes to town to have Joe hanged.

Guest Stars: Joan Freeman, Steve Cochran

Written by: Ken Pettus

Directed by: William Witney

195. Dead and Gone, *April 4, 1965*

Folk singer Hoyt Axton makes his TV debut as guitar-strummin' drifter Howard Mead. Adam prevents him from robbing brother and sister Johann and Hilda Brunners. But Adam is taken by his songs and convinces the Brunners not to press charges. Howard steals from the Ponderosa but Adam gives him yet another chance, a decision he'll regret.

Guest Stars: Hoyt Axton, Susanne Cramer

Written by: Paul Schneider

Directed by: Robert Totten

196. A Good Night's Rest, *April 11, 1965*

Between Joe's flirting, Adam's guitar playing and Hoss' snoring, Ben can't sleep, so he gets a room at the Virginia City hotel. He picks the wrong night; there's a knifing, a lover's quarrel, and a man who keeps wandering into Ben's room.

Guest Stars: Abigail Skelton, Robert Ridgeley, Jean Willes, Lloyd Corrigan, Jay Ripley

Written by: Frank Cleaver, Jeffrey Fleece

Directed by: William F. Claxton

197. To Own the World, *April 18, 1965*

Phenomenally wealthy Charles Hackett wants the Ponderosa by any means necessary. He alienates the only person who ever cared for him, his wife.

Why is Pernell smiling? Could it be because his six-year contract is about to expire?

Guest Stars: Telly Savalas, Linda Lawson

Written by: Ed Adamson

Directed by: Virgil W. Vogel

198. Lothario Larkin, *April 25, 1965*

After a saloon brawl, Roy banishes Lothario Larkin from town and Hoss takes him in. Hoss discovers the source of Lothario's anxiety - the woman he loves is spoken for.

Guest Stars: Noah Beery Jr., Dorothy Green

Written by: Warren Douglas

Directed by: William Witney

199. The Return, *May 2, 1965*

When ex-convict Trace Cordell returns, banker Paul Dorn feels threatened. Trace crippled Paul in a gun-fight years ago, and Paul is now married to Trace's former sweetheart Clara. Paul fears she might leave him; she married him out of pity.

Guest Stars: Tony Young, Joan Blackman, John Conte, Robert J. Stevenson, Dan Riss, Phil Chambers, Bill Clark

Written by: Ken Pettus, Frank Chase

Directed by: Virgil W. Vogel

200. The Jonah, *May 9, 1965*

New ranch hand George has the reputation of a jinx. Hoss tries to convince him not to pay any attention, but even he's frightened when a gypsy predicts events ending in death, and the events start happening.

Guest Stars: Angela Clark, Erin O'Donnell, Dean Harens, Andrew Prine, Ken Mayer, Troy Melton

Written by: Preston Wood

Directed by: William Claxton

201. The Spotlight, *May 16, 1965*

Ben is entertainment coordinator for Virginia City's anniversary ceremonies. Retired opera singer Angela Drake comes to the Ponderosa. She lost her voice years before, but she tells Ben she can't sing without perfect accompaniment. Ben is ecstatic when her former accompanist arrives, but Angela is not. Carleton left her to become a renowned pianist.

Guest Stars: Viveca Lindfors, Ron Randell, Robert Foulk, Winnie Coffin, John Fredericks, Ian Wolfe, Jeanne Detterman, Billy M. Greene

Written by: Dick Carr

Directed by: Gerd Oswald

202. Patchwork Man, *May 23, 1965*

Hoss hires recluse Patch, who makes great apple pie. Ben is unimpressed when Patch cowers during a fight with a mining boss. He must overcome a fear of violence stemming from his teen years.

Guest Stars: Grant Williams, Bruce Gordon, Sue Randall, Lane Bradford

Season 7

203. The Debt, *September 12, 1965*

Wiley and Annie Kane request unpaid jobs. Their father Sam had stolen from Ben, and Wiley lives in disgrace. They had thought Sam was dead, but he appears and Annie breaks him out of jail. Joe must prevent Wiley from killing Sam.

Guest Stars: Tommy Sands, Brooke Bundy

Written by: William Blinn

Directed by: William F. Claxton

204. The Dilemma, *September 19, 1965*

Ben becomes acting judge just before the bank is robbed and the town faces ruin. The only man who could have cracked the safe is old Sundown Davis, who Ben helped get paroled. Sundown says the money is well hidden. He will return it and save the town if Ben lets him go.

Guest Stars: Tom Tully, Anthony Call

Written by: John and Ward Hawkins

Directed by: William Claxton

205. The Brass Box,
September 26, 1965

Although no one ever believes him, old Jose Ortega is always telling tall tales, including one about a Spanish land grant giving him ownership of the territory.

Guest Stars: Ramon Novarro, Michael Dante

Written by: Paul Schneider

Directed by: William Claxton

206. The Other Son,
October 3, 1965

The mines are flooded, ruining the town. Ben writes Adam who suggests nitroglycerin. Ben hires Clint Watson and his sons Andy and Ellis to transport the explosives. Clint favors his older son Andy. When Andy is killed, Clint blames Ellis. He says he killed Andy just like he killed his mother during childbirth.

Guest Stars: Ed Begley, Bing Russell, Tom Simcox

Written by: Thomas Thompson

Directed by: William F. Claxton

207. The Lonely Runner, *October 10, 1965*

Jim Acton sold a herd of wild horses to Sam Whipple, and Sam claims that Jim's prized mare was part of the deal. The judge awards Sam the mare. When Acton later tries to strike a deal, Sam shoots at him, and Acton kills Sam in self defense. The Cartwrights know he's innocent but can't persuade him to face charges; Jim needs to run free.

Guest Stars: Gilbert Roland, Pat Conway, Ken Lynch

Written by: Thomas Thompson

Directed by: William Witney

Dan Blocker clowns around with former teacher Freda Gibson Powell and friend Dennis Reed, also Freda's former student

The Cartwrights continue, minus one. The cast and crew were concerned that Bonanza might not survive after Pernell Roberts' departure but in fact, it enjoyed its greatest success in those later seasons.

208. Devil on Her Shoulder,
October 17, 1965

The Reverend Evan Morgan's wife is convinced Morgan's niece, Sarah Reynolds, is Satan's daughter. Sarah had grown up with the brethren but left. When her husband and child died she rejoined, bringing outside ideas. One of the group's women is dying of cholera. Morgan's wife thinks the woman became infected from a flower Sarah gave her. When the epidemic kills Morgan's wife, he feels he must burn his niece at the stake.

Guest Stars: Ina Balin, John Doucette

Written by: Suzanne Clauser

Directed by: Virgil W. Vogel

209. Found Child, *October 24, 1965*

Hoss finds a young girl, the only survivor of a stagecoach robbery. Her uncle comes for her, but he orchestrated the robbery in the first place. The girl's parents had hidden valuable documents in her doll. Her uncle plans to take the doll and kill his neice.

Guest Stars: Eileen Baral, Gerald Mohr

Written by: Frank Cleaver

Directed by: Ralph E. Black

210. The Meredith Smith,
October 31, 1965

With stingy Jake Smith's dying breath he instructs Ben to give his estate to Meredith Smith. Ben puts an ad in the paper for Meredith. If he doesn't appear the estate reverts to the territory. This would be bad; Ben had been leasing water rights from Jake. The day before the deadline, six people claim to be Meredith. Ben must discover the truth or lose the water rights.

Guest Stars: Strother Martin, Anne Helm, Robert Colbert, Burt Mustin

Written by: Lois Hire

Directed by: John Florea

211. Mighty Is the Word,
November 7, 1965

Former gunfighter Paul Watson is now a preacher, but Cliff Rexford can't forgive him for killing his brother 5 years ago. Rexford destroys the Watsons' nearly-completed church. Watson won't respond with violence. But then Rexford drags Watson's wife into the conflict.

Guest Stars: Glenn Corbett, Michael Whitney, Sue Randall

Written by: Thomas Thompson, Robert L. Goodwin

Directed by: William F. Claxton

212. The Strange One, *November 14, 1965*

A wagon train abandons one of their members, Marie. Her family think she's a witch. She touches Joe's mother's music box and knows all about the Cartwrights. A diphtheria epidemic Marie had predicted hits, and even her mother and father want her hanged. This episode is now shown on USA network as a movie with *Second Sight*, also about a psychic.

Guest Stars: Louise Sorel, Robert McQueeney, Willard Sage

Written by: Jo Pagano, Stephen Lord

Directed by: Gerd Oswald

213. The Reluctant Rebel,
November 21, 1965

Billy Penn is ashamed of his father, a pig farmer. He joins a gang of rustlers but is caught stealing Cartwright cattle. Hoss knows Billy needs to feel important. He puts Billy in charge of a bull that he plans to enter in the fair.

Guest Stars: Tim Considine, Royal Dano

Written by: Wally George

Directed by: R.G. Springsteen

214. Five Sundowns to Sunup,
December 5, 1965

Harry Lassiter is in jail awaiting hanging. His mother has her other son, Carver, kidnap one citizen each night for five nights, and hang them if Harry isn't released. When Joe is kidnapped, Ben wonders if he should risk five people to see justice done.

Guest Stars: Marie Windsor, Douglas Henderson, John Hoyt

Written by: William L. Stuart

Directed by: Gerd Oswald

215. A Natural Wizard, *December 12, 1965*

Skeeter Dexter sets animals free from his stepfather's traps. Skeeter's drunken stepfather is furious and leaves. With his stepfather gone, the Cartwrights encourage Skeeter to live with his mother. His mother wants nothing to do with him. She says he forced her to marry first his father and then his stepfather when his father deserted.

Guest Stars: Eddie Hodges, Douglas Kennedy, Jacqueline Scott

Written by: William Blinn, Suzanne Clauser

Directed by: Robert Totten

216. All Ye His Saints, *December 19, 1965*

When young Michael Thorpe's father is wounded, an Indian named Lijah tells him only God can save his father, and that He lives on the mountain. The boy goes to the mountain. Joe finds him, and the two find old hermit Caine, who Michael thinks is God. Caine says he'll heal Michael's father if the boy promises total obedience.

Guest Stars: Clint Howard, Leif Erickson

Written by: William Blinn

Directed by: William F. Claxton

217. A Dublin Lad, *January 2, 1966*

Irishman Terrence O'Toole is accused of murder, and Joe is hesitant to find him guilty. A guilty verdict is finally reached, but Joe is still not sure. With a matter of hours until the hanging, Joe seeks the truth, angering the murdered man's widow, who was once engaged to Terrence.

Guest Stars: Liam Sullivan, Maggie Mahoney

Written by: Mort Thaw

Directed by: William F. Claxton

218. To Kill A Buffalo, *January 9, 1966*

Hoss finds a wounded Indian and brings him back to the Ponderosa. His name is Tatoo, and his tribe left him when he was injured. With his tribe gone, Hoss tries to find him a new identity as a white man.

Guest Stars: Jose De Vega, Steven Gravers

Written by: Michael Fisher

Directed by: William F. Claxton

219. Ride the Wind (Part I), *January 16, 1966*

Charles Ludlow starts the Pony Express. Chief Winnemuca threatens to kill anyone who crosses his land, which lies on part of the route. Ludlow wants peace, but assistant Curtis Wade wants to fight. Reporter Tully encourages Wade. Ludlow is killed delivering a treaty.

Guest Stars: Victor Jory, Rod Cameron, DeForest Kelley

Written by: Paul Schneider

Directed by: William Witney

220. Ride the Wind (Part II), *January 23, 1966*

Charles Ludlow's son Jabey gets drunk and Curtis Wade takes over the Pony Express. Wade wants to violently stop the Indian threat, and Jabey is too drunk and depressed to stop him.

Guest Stars: Same as above

Written by: Paul Schneider

Directed by: William Witney

221. Destiny's Child, *January 30, 1966*

Sonny is even bigger than Hoss, but has a child's mind. He and Jessie Pherson are on their way to Oregon, but are short of money. Ben finds Jessie a job horse breaking. When he's killed, Sonny is inconsolable and runs off for Oregon. Sheriff Roy Coffee discovers Sonny is wanted for an Arizona murder, and Roy must form a posse to bring him back.

Guest Stars: Dick Peabody, Walter Burke

Written by: Robert Barron

Directed by: Gerd Oswald

222. Peace Officer, *February 6, 1966*

With Sheriff Coffee in St. Louis, the Morissey bunch wreck the saloon. They accidentally kill Deputy Bill Harris. All escape except Cliff, who is jailed. Mayor Garrett hires Wes Dunn as temporary sheriff. Wes badly beats Cliff. Joe thinks Dunn is a hero until he sees him murder another suspect.

Guest Stars: Eric Fleming, Ron Foster

Written by: Donn Mullally

Directed by: William Witney

223. The Code, *February 13, 1966*

Dan Taggert baits Joe into a duel, while an Englishman named Fitts takes bets. Joe tries unsuccessfully to reason with Taggert. Joe shoots Taggert in the arm. He discovers he was a pawn; Taggert and Fitts travel together taking bets on duels.

Guest Stars: George Montgomery, Robert Ellenstein

Written by: Sidney Ellis

Directed by: William F. Claxton

224. Three Brides for Hoss, *February 20, 1966*

Three women each claim Hoss sent for her to be his bride. The group - a widow from Kentucky; a dame from New Orleans; and an intellectual New-Englander – all have letters describing the Ponderosa. Ben discovers the culprit is a widower with a young daughter in need of a mother.

Guest Stars: Stuart Erwin, Wynn Pearce

Written by: Jo Pagano

Directed by: Ralph E. Black

225. The Emperor Norton, *February 27, 1966*

Joshua Norton is an eccentric old man and "Emperor of the United States of America and the Protector of Mexico". He wants to improve mine safety. The mine owners try to prove Norton insane. Ben and Norton's other friends, including Mark Twain, must prove otherwise.

Guest Stars: Sam Jaffe, Parley Baer

Written by: Robert Sabaroff, Gerry P. Young

Directed by: William F. Claxton

226. Her Brother's Keeper,
March 6, 1966

Ben's romance with Claire Armory is complicated by her brother, Carl, an invalid who relies on sympathy to use people.

Guest Stars: Nancy Gates, Wesley Lau

Written by: Mort Thaw, Lee Pickett

Directed by: Virgil W. Vogel

227. The Trouble With Jamie,
March 20, 1966

Ben's cousin Matthew brings his son Jamie to the Ponderosa and leaves for San Francisco with his ward, Elizabeth. Jamie is a brat, but during his stay Ben turns him into a man. When his father and Elizabeth return and announce their engagement, Jamie is heartbroken – he has always loved Elizabeth.

Guest Stars: Michael Burns, Ross Elliott

Written by: Helen B. Hicks

Directed by: R.G. Springsteen

228. Shining In Spain,
March 27, 1966

Wendy Daniels comes to town to meet up with her father, Taylor. The Cartwrights realize something's wrong when her supposedly rich father leaves her stranded. When she is evicted from the hotel, she goes to the Ponderosa, only to have her dreams shattered when her father shows up broke.

Guest Stars: Judi Rolin, Woodrow Parfrey

Written by: Elliott Gilbert

Directed by: Maury Geraghty

229. The Genius, *April 3, 1966*

Will Smith is an alcoholic poet who entertains folks with his colorful poetry. He has run from his wife. When she finds him she tells Hoss that Smith is really famous poet William Warlock Evans, and she is determined to sober him up.

Guest Star: Lonny Chapman

Where's Adam? This was an early photo of all four Cartwrights, with Adam standing between Hoss and Joe. He was airbrushed out.

Written by: Donn Mullally

Directed by: R.G. Springsteen

230. The Unwritten Commandment,
April 10, 1966

Willard Walker is not impressed with his son's talent; he says the boy should be doing more chores and less singing. Wayne Newton fans are treated to four songs: *Old Joe Clark, Scarlett Ribbons, Danny Boy* and *The Old Rugged Cross*.

Guest Stars: Wayne Newton, Anne Jeffreys, Malcolm Atterbury

Written by: Jo Pagano, William Blinn, Dan Ullman

Directed by: Gerd Oswald

231. Big Shadows on the Land,
April 17, 1966

Italian immigrant Giorgio Rossi and his family settle on the Ponderosa. Giorgio insists in America you are free to take what you like. Ben relents and decides to give him the worthless land; the water is alkali poisoned. Giorgio knows how to purify the water, and Ben feels his secret is a fair exchange.

Guest Stars: Jack Kruschen, Brioni Farrell

Written by: William F. Leicester, Richard H. Bartlett

Directed by: William F. Claxton

232. The Fighters, *April 24, 1966*

Boxers Charlie Powers and Hank Kelly and promoter Ross Dugan visit Virginia City. Hoss injures Hank, and the doctor prohibits Hank from fighting.

Dugan offers Hank's wife help if she gets Hoss to fight Charlie. Hoss refuses, but Ross and Charlie humiliate him until he fights.

Guest Stars: Philip Pine, Michael Conrad

Written by: Robert L. Goodwin

Directed by: R.G. Springsteen

233. Home From the Sea,
May 1, 1966

The Cartwrights are visited by Adam's shipmate Gilly Maples. He and his accomplice stole letters from Adam, in which Ben detailed a large gold payment. Gilly and his accomplice plan to steal the gold, but now Gilly has second thoughts.

Guest Stars: Alan Bermann, Ivor Barry

Written by: George F. Slavin, Stanley Adams

Directed by: Jean Yarbrough

234. The Last Mission,
May 8, 1966

Ben and Hoss accompany Ben's friend Colonel Keith Jarrell to talk peace with the Paiutes. Corporal Poker tells Hoss about the massacre that killed his family. Poker is killed, and Hoss suspects he was purposely given a dangerous job.

Guest Stars: R.G. Armstrong, Tom Reese

Written by: William Douglas Lansford, S.S. Schweitzer

Directed by: R.G. Springsteen

235. A Dollar's Worth of Trouble,
May 15, 1966

Fortune teller Madame Adella says she sees a tall blonde who will fall in love with Hoss. Joe thinks its hilarious until Hoss meets Kathleen Walker. Then Adella tells Hoss to fear Craig Bonner, who has killed 13 men. But Bonner is now nearsighted, and the only thing he's shot lately is his foot.

Guest Stars: Sally Kellerman, Mabel Anderson, Elisha Cook

Written by: Robert L. Goodwin

Directed by: Don Daves

Season 8

236. Something Hurt, Something Wild, *September 11, 1966*

Jed Ferguson's daughter Laurie has come home after six years of school back East, and she and Joe are starting a romance. But she screams when Joe kisses her and claims he attacked her. The Fergusons build a fence on their property, and Jed's son Cleve threatens to shoot any Cartwright who crosses it. The Cartwrights wonder why Laurie did what she did.

Guest Stars: Lyle Bettger, Lynn Loring

Written by: William R. Cox

Directed by: William Witney

237. Horse of a Different Hue, *September 18, 1966*

Colonel Fairchild and his granddaughter challenge Joe to race his horse Clancy against their Jeff Davis. The Fairchilds owe money to Jack Geller, who bullies a $5,000 bet out of Joe. When Ben tries to cancel the bet, Geller persuades him to double it. Geller forces the Colonel to dye a faster horse named Lightnin' to look like Jeff Davis. To top it off, the Colonel knows if Joe wins, Geller will kill the Cartwrights.

Guest Stars: Charles Ruggles, Skip Homeier, Julie Parrish

Written by: William R. Cox

Directed by: William Witney

238. A Time to Step Down, *September 25, 1966*

Wrangler Dan Tolliver is too old for dangerous work. He quits when Ben tries to give him an easier job. Dan forgets his longtime friendship with Ben and joins two outlaws planning to rob the Ponderosa.

Guest Stars: Ed Begley, Audrey Totter, Donald "Red" Barry, Sherwood Price, Reny McEvoy, Bruno Ve Soto

Written by: Frank Chase

Directed by: Paul Heinreid

239 & 240. See "Lost Episodes"

241. To Bloom for Thee, *October 16, 1966*

Within four days of meeting, Hoss and unfriendly Carol Attley are planning to marry. But when she has dinner with the Cartwrights she won't reveal anything about herself. She later tells Hoss she accidentally killed her abusive husband. When the U.S. marshal comes looking for her, Ben learns the killing was no accident and she was having an affair at the time.

Guest Stars: Geraldine Brooks, Don Haggerty

Written by: June Randolph

Directed by: Sutton Roley

242. Credit for a Kill, *October 23, 1966*

Joe and his friend Morgan Tanner shoot at a horse thief simultaneously, but only one bullet hits and kills him. Morgan, a poor rancher, doesn't know why Joe is taking the credit and the large reward. Joe doesn't tell anyone the thief's brother is looking for revenge.

Guest Stars: Don Collier, Dean Harens, Charles Maxwell, Regina Gleason, Ed Faulkner, Ted Markland

Written by: Fredric Louis Fox

Directed by: William Claxton

243. Four Sisters From Boston, *October 30, 1966*

The four Lowell sisters inherit the Landcastle ranch, and a $2,800 tax bill. Ben owes a debt to their late uncle, so at the property auction he pays the tax bill. The Lowells actually owed far less money. Two cattlemen, Catlin and Billings, rigged the auction to get the land. Sarah Lowell is suspicious of Ben; she thinks he wants to take over the Landcastle ranch. When Catlin and Billings burn their shed and poison their water, Sarah thinks Ben is the villain.

Guest Stars: Vera Miles, Morgan Woodward, Kay Edgington, Melinda Plowman, Rand Brooks, Owen Bush

Written by: John M. Chester

Directed by: Alan Crossland, Jr.

244. Old Charlie, *November 6, 1966*

Charlie is an old man who tells tales. Drifter Billy Barker tries to rob him at knifepoint. After he knocks Charlie out, Hoss punches Billy and accidentally kills him with the knife. When Charlie wakes up he tells everyone he killed Billy, prompting Billy's brothers George and Jack to seek revenge.

Guest Stars: John McIntire, Jeanette Nolan, Tim McIntire, Bill Fletcher, Hal Baylor, Bruno Ve Soto, Dick Winslow

Written by: Robert and Wanda Duncan

Directed by: William Claxton

245. Ballad of the Ponderosa, *November 13, 1966*

Fifteen years ago, Ben's testimony at Doug Preston's murder trial convicted Preston. Preston broke out of jail and was lynched. Doug's son Colter is now a balladeer, and he comes to town singing a song denouncing Ben. Then he fakes a beating to convince people to reconsider the case. Finally he shoots himself in the stomach and claims Ben did it to silence him. Only the widow of the man who was murdered fifteen years ago can save Ben with the truth.

Guest Stars: Randy Boone, Ann Doran, Roger Davis, John Archer

Written by: Michael Landon, Rik Vollaerts

Directed by: William F. Claxton

246. The Oath, *November 20, 1966*

Half-breed Charlie Two's father is hanged; before the execution he makes Charlie swear to kill Ben. While on his way to the Ponderosa, Charlie meets Joe and, without knowing who he is, tells him the plan. Joe conceals his identity and tries to make Charlie change his mind.

Guest Stars: Tony Bill, Douglas Kennedy

Written by:

Directed by:

247. A Real Nice, Friendly Little Town, *November 27, 1966*

Joe is hit in the butt with a ricocheting bullet, and Hoss must catch the culprit. It is one of two identical twins, Judd and Jeb Rikeman, who, along with mother Mae, give him a hard time.

Guest Stars: Louise Latham, Mark Slade, Robert Doyle, Robert Foulk, Burt Mustin, Herb Vigran, Billy M. Greene, Clegg Hoyt, Vaughn Taylor

Written by: Herman Hoffman

Directed by: Herman Hoffman

248. The Bridegroom, *December 4, 1966*

Maggie Dowling's father often reminds her she is plain. When he offers to pay off a widower's ranch if he marries her, she is mortified. Joe convinces her to stop pitying herself. The two pretend Joe is courting her to make the widower jealous.

Guest Stars: Ron Hayes, Joanne Linville

Written by: Walter Black

Directed by: William F. Claxton

249. Tommy, *December 18, 1966*

Allie's father was Ben's foreman. Now she appears with her deaf mute son Tommy. Her husband and Tommy's stepfather, Jess Miller, just broke out of jail. Jess wants to take Allie to Mexico, leaving Tommy behind. Allie and Tommy take refuge at the Ponderosa, but when Jess shoots Joe in the back, she decides to go to Mexico before he does any more damage.

Guest Stars: Teddy Quinn, Janet DeGore

Written by: Mort Thaw, Mary T. Taylor, Thomas Thompson

Directed by: William Witney

250. A Christmas Story, *December 25, 1966*

Andy Walker comes home to sing at the orphans' benefit. His father has died, and he now travels with his uncle/manager Thadeus Cade. Thadeus wants to tour with Andy, taking 10% for himself. Meanwhile, Hoss must raise $20,000 for the benefit. He hires Thadeus Cade, who promises to raise it in exchange for 10%, causing Andy to rethink his greedy uncle.

Guest Stars: Wayne Newton, Jack Oakie

Written by: Thomas Thompson

Directed by: Gerd Oswald

251. Ponderosa Explosion, *January 1, 1967*

Hoss and Joe spend $50 on two common rabbits,

thinking they are a non-existent breed called "Derby Royal". They want to supply women with Derby Royal fur coats. Their problems multiply faster than the rabbits when they haven't got the heart to skin the cute little animals; and they sold a third share of the business in exchange for a horse for Ben's birthday.

Guest Stars: Dub Taylor, Chick Chandler

Written by: Alex Sharp

Directed by: William F. Claxton

252. Justice, *January 8, 1967*

Joe and Sally the bank teller are engaged; the two don't notice that Sally's shy co-worker Horace is obsessed with her. When Sally ignores him he tries to restrain her, killing her accidentally. A distraught Joe must proove Horace's guilt, following him every moment until he confesses.

Guest Star: Beau Bridges

Written by: Richard Wendley

Directed by: Lewis Allen

253. A Bride for Buford, *January 15, 1967*

Grubby miner Buford Buckalaw and his brother have just struck gold, and they celebrate. The saloon is graced by Dolly Brantree, whom every man in Virginia City would love to have. When her crooked manager finds out about Buford's, he forces Dolly to fake an attraction to him. Hoss dresses up as a society man to turn Dolly's attention away from Buford and see if she's interested in him or his money.

Guest Stars: Lola Albright, Jack Elam

Written by: Robert V. Barron

Directed by: William F. Claxton

254. Black Friday, *January 22, 1967*

Joe comes across former ranch hand turned gunfighter, Friday. Friday is ill and stranded in a town where Judge Wylitt is planning an unfair gunfight for him at the end of the week. Friday killed Judge Wylitt's son in a gunfight, and the judge has sought revenge ever since. Joe tries to nurse Friday back to health so he'll have a fair shot in the duel.

Guest Stars: John Saxon, Ford Rainey

Written by: Herbert Kastle, John Hawkins

Directed by: William F. Claxton

255. The Unseen Wound, *January 29, 1967*

Ben goes to Concho to visit old friend Paul Rowan, and is surprised when he must check his gun in Paul's office. Paul has outlawed guns in Concho. Paul's deputy and the town eccentric are killed in a gunfight. Paul snaps and barricades himself in a warehouse, shooting into the street. The people of Concho want to kill Paul quickly, but Ben tries to help him. Leslie Nielsen was one of Lorne Greene's students at his Academy of Radio Arts, and the two remained close.

Guest Stars: Leslie Nielsen, Nancy Malone, Percy Helton, Douglas Henderson

Written by: Frank Chase

Directed by: Gerd Oswald

256. Journey to Terror, *February 5, 1967*

Joe visits his friends Tom and Ellie Sue Blackwell and their son. They have been hit by a drought. Joe learns that Tom has been out looking for work. Tom returns followed by outlaw Wade Hollister, his girlfriend Rita and Wade's critically ill father. They hold Joe and the Blackwells prisoner and demand care for Wade's sick father. Ellie Sue doesn't know her husband has been with the outlaws for a long time.

Guest Stars: John Ericson, Jason Evers, Kevin Hagen, Lindsay Workman, Elizabeth Rogers, Lory Patrick, Richard Hale

Written by: Joel Murcott

Directed by: Lewis Allen

257. Amigo, *February 12, 1967*

Amigo is a downtrodden Mexican riding with a terrorist band. After Ben saves his life, a hot-headed Joe wants to see him hanged, but realizes his mistake after Amigo proves he's trustworthy.

Guest Stars: Henry Darrow, Gregory Walcott, Anna Navarro, Warren Kemmerling, Tim Herbert, Grandon Rhodes

Written by: John Hawkins, Jack Turley

Directed by: William Claxton

258. A Woman in the House,
February 19, 1967

Russ Wharton applies for roundup work at the Ponderosa. Ben is just about to turn away the drunk when Russ says he's Mary Farnum's husband. Mary has been a friend of the Cartwrights for many years. Ben gives Russ a job and a cabin out of pity for Mary. When Ben sees Russ beating Mary, he takes her back with him and doesn't allow Russ to see her. But Mary's convinced that Ben is in love with her.

Guest Stars: Diane Baker, Paul Richards

Written by: Joel Murcott

Directed by: Gerd Oswald

259. Judgment at Red Creek, February 26, 1967

When Sheriff Rimbau's brother and friend are murdered at the Red Creek station, Rimbau plans revenge, without a trial. Joe joins the posse to ensure the prisoners get to Virginia City safely for their trial. Before long, they find two drifters that fit the description, and Joe has a hard time ensuring their safety.

Guest Stars: John Ireland, Harry Carey, James Sikking, Bartlett Robinson, John Raymer, Martin West

Written by: Robert Sabaroff

Directed by: William Claxton

260. Joe Cartwright, Detective, March 5, 1967

Joe has been reading British whodunnit novels, and is fascinated by Scotland Yard techniques. In the bank,, he overhears two strangers asking about the reliability of the safe. He immediately recognizes the situation from his book *How to Solve Crimes* as a key way to recognize a bank robber. He and Hoss try to warn Clem, but Clem, of course laughs at them. With no support from the law or their father, they set out to catch the criminals on their own, with hilarious results.

Guest Stars: Mort Mills, Ken Lynch, Bing Russell

Written by: Michael Landon, Oliver Crawford

Directed by: William F. Claxton

261. Dark Enough to See the Stars, March 12, 1967

Ben offers young drifter Billy Wilcox a job. When Mr. Yardley and his daughter Jennifer visit, Jennifer falls in love with Billy. But Billy is too nervous about the Yardleys' traveling companion, a lawman, to notice Jennifer. Billy's real name is Aaron, and he is wanted in his corrupt hometown. The town boss killed his mother, and was acquitted. After that, he got into a gunfight with Aaron, who killed him in self-defense.

Guest Stars: Richard Evans, Linda Foster

Written by: Kelly Covin

Directed by: Don Daves

262. The Deed and the Dilemma, March 26, 1967

Giorgio Rossi's dream comes true when Ben gives him a land grant for 80 acres. Now, with his water purification process perfected, he can grow grapes for his "Vino de Ponderosa". But Rossi's happiness is short-lived. The water runs through Cass Gurney's property, and Cass and his foreman, Jim Blake take advantage of the immigrant family.

This episode was a pilot to a series that never happened.

Guest Stars: Jack Kruschen, Donald Woods

Written by: William F. Leicester

Directed by: William F. Claxton

263. The Prince, April 2, 1967

International intrigue comes to the Ponderosa when the Cartwrights welcome Russian Count Alexis and Countess Elena, unaware that an outlaw is planning a reception of his own.

Guest Stars: Lloyd Bochner, Claire Griswold

Written by: John Hawkins, Melvin Levy

Directed by: William F. Claxton

264. A Man Without Land, April 9, 1967

Ben's neighbor Matt Jeffers is in financial trouble. One corner of his ranch is irrigated by the Ponderosa; the rest is bone dry, and he is forced to turn it over to the first man who can pay the back taxes. His foreman wants the land. But when Ben agrees to get Matt back on his feet, the foreman becomes obsessed with the land. The plan? To drive a giant wedge between Matt and Ben. While Joe is hunting deer on the Jeffers ranch, the foreman kills Matt's son, framing Joe.

Guest Stars: Jeremy Slate, Royal Dano, Joan Marshall, Dorothy Neumann

Written by: Steve McNeil

Directed by: Don Daves

265. Napoleon's Children, *April 16, 1967*

The young nephew of a drunken ex-professor, who thinks of himself as the great strategist Napoleon, leads a band of tough kids in a terrorizing crime wave. When one of their "soldiers" is caught stealing horses and arrested, Napoleon drills his army to get the boy out of jail. They nearly succeed, stealing guns and ammunition from right under everyone's noses. But Joe finds Napoleon's tragic flaw; he's really a coward who takes shelter in his command post during battle.

Guest Stars: Michael Burns, Robert Biheller, Phyllis Hill, Woodrow Parfrey

Written by: Judith and Robert Guy Barrows

Directed by: Christian Nyby

266. The Wormwood Cup, *April 23, 1967*

Joe is absolved of murder when a coroner's inquest determines he shot in self-defense. The dead man's father wanted to see Joe hanged. Then a woman comes to Virginia City offering $1,000 to anyone who kills Joe in a fair fight. She is convinced that Joe killed her brother in a separate case.

Guest Stars: Frank Overton, Judi Meredith, Will J. White, Myron Healey, Bruno Ve Soto, Robert B. Williams

Written by: Michael Landon, Joy Dexter

Directed by: William Claxton

267. Clarissa, *April 30, 1967*

The Cartwrights ask for trouble when they welcome their snobbish Eastern cousin Clarissa. She wastes no time making trouble and alienating most of their friends.

Guest Stars: Nina Foch, Roy Roberts

Written by: Chester Krumholz

Directed by: Lewis Allen

268. Maestro Hoss, *May 7, 1967*

Madame Marova, a palm-reading con woman convinces gullible Hoss that he is a musical genius. She sells him an old fiddle, claiming it's a Stradivarius, and tells him he'll give his first concert within a week. He believes her faithfully, paying no attention to his father and brother, who mistake his playing for a wounded animal.

Guest Stars: Zsa Zsa Gabor, Kathleen Freeman

Written by: U.S. Andersen

Directed by: William F. Claxton

269. The Greedy Ones, *May 14, 1967*

When Gus Schultz finally strikes it rich after thirty years, Virginia City is thrown into chaos. The Cartwrights fear that Gus made his strike on the Ponderosa, and that they will be overrun by greedy gold-seekers. A mining tycoon named Shasta offers Schultz $15,000 and a 30% share of the gold for exclusive mining rights, but Schultz refuses. Shasta will do anything to get that mine. When a partnership attempt with Ben fails, Shasta offers a reward to

Joe defeats the self-proclaimed Napoleon in "Napoleon's Children"

anyone who can locate the mine. Ben vows to keep all prospectors off the Ponderosa even if it means involving the Army.

Guest Stars: *Robert Middleton, George Chandler, Lane Bradford, William Bakewell, Phil Chambers, Grandon Rhodes*

Written by: *James Amesbury*

Directed by: *Don Daves*

Ben contemplates his mortality in "To Die In Darkness"

Hoss and Joe have their hands full in "Little Girl Lost"

The excitement continues to build in "Salute to Yesterday"

International intrigue comes to the Ponderosa in "The Prince"

Ben offers his sympathies in "Showdown at Tahoe"

The two-part episode "Ride the Wind" was released as a feature film in foreign countries.
This is a lobby card from Mexico.

A very rare board game from Germany. The instructions, of course, are entirely in German.

To take his mind off the Hollywood "snobbery", Dan Blocker was a partner in Vinegaroon Racing Associates.
Here, a driver visits him on the set.

An aerial shot of the wonderful episode "To Die in Darkness"

The Cartwrights and Candy face life sentences for trespassing in "Kingdom of Fear"

Dan Blocker and John Mitchum made a wonderful record of folk songs, available on the Bear Family set

This page: Aladdin Industries lunch box from 1963. Next two pages: Lunch boxes from 1965 and 1968. Notice the Adam-like character on the 1965; it was manufactured when NBC was unsure about Pernell Roberts' future with the show.

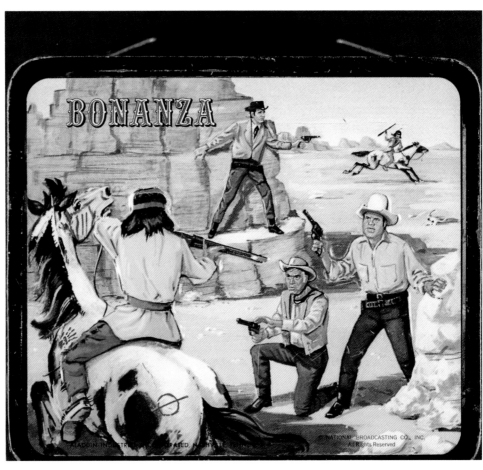

Michael Landon never considered retiring after Bonanza. Here, he poses with his "Little House on the Prairie" family.

Pernell Roberts returned to series T.V. in 1979 for "Trapper John, M.D." for CBS, which ran until 1986

Victor French made several guest appearances on Bonanza, and he and Landon became lifelong friends. This is a publicity photo from their popular show "Highway to Heaven".

SEASON 9

270. Second Chance, *September 17, 1967*

Joe is hit with an Indian arrow. Hoss tries to remove the arrow, but it breaks, leaving the arrowhead deep in Joe's shoulder. They're forced to take refuge in a mismatched wagon train camp, composed of two women, two thieves, a dying man and a coward. Unlike other wagon trains, these people have had enough of the West, and are now headed back East. This script was originally titled "The Losers".

Guest Stars: James Gregory, Joe De Santis, Bettye Ackerman, Douglas Kennedy, Olan Soule, Jane Zachary

Written by: John Hawkins, Paul Sneider

Directed by: Leon Benson

271. Sense of Duty, *September 24, 1967*

Ben commands a militia unit escorting a rabble-rousing Indian to prison. On the way, they encounter the prisoner's loyal followers led by Chief Winnemuca. They feel the prisoner is a god, and will stop at nothing to protect him.. Chief Winnemuca even puts aside his friendship with Ben and orders his warriors to fight the militia. Candy (David Canary) makes his first appearance as a drifter looking for a meal and an adventure.

Guest Stars: Gene Rutherford, Michael Forest, Ron Foster, Richard Hale

Written by: John Hawkins, Gil Lasky

Directed by: William Witney

272. The Conquistadors, *October 1, 1967*

A band of Mexicans kidnaps Joe and demands a ransom of $25,000 in gold. Ben pays it, but Joe is not out of danger. A group of white outlaws hear about the gold. While Joe and the Mexicans are fighting off the new outlaws, Joe develops sympathy for the down-trodden Mexicans. Their soil back home is poisoned with lye, and their people are starving.

Guest Stars: John Saxon, Eddie Ryder, John Kellogg, Mike De Anda, Brooke Bundy, Arch Johnson, Dabbs Greer, James Griffith, Robert Brubaker, Rusty Lane, Vaughn Taylor, Olan Soule

Written by: Walter Black

Directed by: John Rich

273. Judgment at Olympus, *October 8, 1967*

Candy desperately needs Hoss and Joe's help when he's charged with murder in Olympus. He is accused of murdering a man who he had fought with shortly before. His defense attorney is paid by the victim's father, and there is an alleged eye-witness who will say anything for drinking money.

Guest Star: Barry Sullivan

Written by: Walter Black

Directed by: John Rich

274. Night of Reckoning, *October 15, 1967*

A band of outlaws inflict a night of terror on the Ponderosa trying to retrieve holdup money from their double-crossing partner who is lying wounded in the Cartwright house.

Guest Stars: Richard Jaeckel, Ron Hayes, Joan Freeman, Teno Pollock, William Jordan, Grandon Rhodes

Written by: Walter Black

Directed by: Leon Benson

275. False Witness, *October 22, 1967*

Hoss, Joe, Candy and Valerie Townsend are put under 24-hour protection by the Sheriff of Sand Dust. They have witnessed a murder, and the brothers of the accused killer want to make sure they don't live to testify. Although they're under constant threat, the boys find time to fight over Valerie, who is too scared to testify.

Guest Stars: Davey Davison, Michael Blodgett, Robert McQueeney, Bill Fletcher, Russ Conway, Frank Gerstle

Written by: Eric Norden

Directed by: Michael Moore

276. The Gentle Ones, *October 29, 1967*

Ben hires Mark Cole as a horsebreaker, even though Mark is perceived as a coward. But Ben is scheduled to sell horses to the army, and he knows about Mark's great gift with animals. Mark's brother, Frank, is also trying to sell horses to the army, but he has only one worthy animal, and it's not yet broken. When Mark finds out that his brother is torturing the horse, he must stand up to Frank for the first time.

Guest Stars: *Robert Walker, Jr., Lana Wood, Pat Conway, Stuart Henderson, Douglas Henderson*

Written by: *Frank Chase*

Directed by: *Harry Harris*

277. Desperate Passage, *November 5, 1967*

The Cartwrights fight their way through savage Paiutes with the sole survivors of an Indian massacre: Josh Tanner, who is charged with murder, and Mary Burns, who knows, but can't reveal that he's innocent.

Guest Stars: *Tina Louise, Steve Forrest, Jane Forrest*

Written by: *John Hawkins*

Directed by: *Leon Benson*

278. The Sure Thing, *November 12, 1967*

Trudy Loughlin captures a terrific wild horse. Her drunken father, who would sell anything for liquor money, sells it to Ben for $100. Ben persuades Trudy to ride the horse in the Virginia City Stakes Race. If she wins, she can have the horse and half the prize money when she reaches legal age. But when all bets go to Trudy's horse, a crooked gambler tries to make Trudy throw the race, even threaten her father's life.

Guest Star: *Kim Darby*

Written by: *Sydney Ellis, Robert Vincent Wright*

Directed by: *William Witney*

279. Showdown at Tahoe, *November 19, 1967*

Jamison Fillmore plans to steal a million dollars from Ben's timber operation, then use his paddle wheel steamboat to escape. Fillmore orders Captain Larson to introduce him to Ben as a lumberman from San Francisco. If he complies, Fillmore will pay for Larson's daughter's education. If he doesn't comply, Fillmore will kill him.

Guest Stars: *Richard Anderson, Sheila Larken, Karl Swenson, Kevin Hagen, Christopher Dark*

Written by: *Thomas Thompson*

Directed by: *Gerald Mayer*

280. Six Black Horses, *November 26, 1967*

Ben gets a visit from his old friend, Onie Dugan. Onie tells Ben that he has over $100,000 cash from years of New York business deals. He wants to invest the money anonymously. Ben takes Onie's money and opens up The Cartwright Lumber Company. After Onie is shot, he confesses to Ben that he is conspiring with Boss Tweed and Tamany Hall. Ben is furious that Onie is continuing with his crooked business ventures, until he sees what Onie has up his sleeve.

Guest Stars: *Burgess Meredith, David Lewis, Judy Parker, Richard X. Slattery, Don Haggerty, Hal Baylor*

Written by: *William Jerome, Michael Landon*

Directed by: *Don Daves*

281. Check Rein, *December 3, 1967*

When Jace Frederick is wounded, he sends Hoss to a horse auction in his place to spend up to $500 for a certain horse. Hoss can't understand why anyone would spend $500 for one horse, but he goes anyway. When he gets there, he finds Jace's uncle Bingham prepared to do anything necessary to get that horse. It's no ordinary horse; it has the rare ability to herd wild horses.

Guest Stars: *Patricia Hyland, Ford Rainey, James MacArthur, Charles Maxwell, Robert Karnes*

Written by: *Robert I. Holt and Olney Sherman*

Directed by: *Leon Benson*

282. Justice Deferred, *December 17, 1967*

Hoss's court testimony hangs Frank Scott for murder. Afterwards, he sees an exact lookalike of Frank Scott, a man named Mel Barnes. He is whistling the same tune that was whistled the night of the murder. No one wants to admit a mistake and reopen the case.

Guest Stars: *Simon Oakland, Nina Talbot, Carl Reindel, Shannon Farnum, John Hubbard, Claudia Bryar, Harlan Warde, Tol Avery, Byron Morrow*

Written by: *Jack Miller*

Directed by: *Gerald Maher*

283. The Gold Detector,
December 24, 1967

Hoss' friend has fallen on hard times and is anxious to sell his worthless mine. A man named Higgins claims he's interested in the traces of copper left in the mine. But Hoss isn't convinced the mine is worthless, and orders a gold detector from the Lodestar Manufacturing Company. Higgins can't take any chances that it might work.

Guest Stars: *Wally Cox, Paul Fix, Dub Taylor, Kelly Thordsen*

Written by: *Ward Hawkins*

Directed by: *Don Daves*

284. The Trackers,
January 7, 1968

Culley Mako is released from a five-year prison term. Shortly after, the bank is robbed and the cashier is killed. Ben was the foreman on the jury that convicted Culley five years earlier, based mainly on Sam Bragen's testimony. Culley insists that Bragen lied on the witness stand, but Ben doesn't believe it. But why is Bragen so anxious to hang Culley?

Guest Stars: *Warren Stevens, Bruce Dern, Warren Vanders, Ted Gehring, Robert P. Lieb, James Sikking, Christopher Shea, Arthur Peterson*

Written by: *Louis Bercovitch, Frederic Louis Fox*

Directed by: *Marc Daniels*

285. A Girl Named George,
January 14, 1968

Enos Blessing has embraced photography. Ben commissions a photograph of himself, his sons, and the ranch hands in front of the house. Cato Troxell orders him to doctor the photo of the Ponderosa so that Troxell appears. This would acquit him of the murder he had committed while the picture was being shot.

Guest Stars: *Sheilah Wells, Jack Albertson, Gerald Mohr, Fred Clark, Andy Devine, Steve Raines, Patsy Kelly*

Little Joe rides into Virginia City by himself. Michael Landon directs "To Die In Darkness", which he also wrote.

Written by: *William H. Wright*

Directed by: *Leon Benson*

286. The Thirteenth Man,
January 21, 1968

Detective Marcus Alley is hired to stop rustling. Alley forces suspects to draw, then he shoots them. There are never any witnesses. He goes after Ben's ranch hand, Heath, with a vengeance. Five years ago, he caught Heath and his two friends rustling. He gunned down the two friends, but Heath escaped.

Guest Stars: *Albert Salmi, Richard Carlson, Ken Tobey, Myron Healey, Bill Quinn, Anna Navarro, John Zaremba, Jon Lormer*

Written by: *Walter Black*

Directed by: *Leon Benson*

287. The Burning Sky, *January 28, 1968*

Ben makes enemies after he hires a ranch hand who is married to Moon, a Sioux Indian. A Ponderosa homesteader, a drunk and bitter half-breed, tries to teach his stepson to hate Indians. The boy becomes her friend anyway. When his stepfather finds out, he beats the boy and tries to kill Moon. She shoots him in self-defense, and is forced to hide out at the Ponderosa from an Indian-hating lynch mob.

Guest Stars: Dawn Wells, Michael Murphy, Iron Eyes Cody, Bobby Riha, Victor French, Robert Foulk, Bill Clark

Written by: William H. Wright and Carol Saraceno

Directed by: John Rich

288. The Price of Salt, *February 4, 1968*

The local cattle are dying due to a terrible salt shortage. Ada Halle in Spanish Wells has a monopoly on salt, and she takes full advantage by raising the price. When a cattle king makes a secret deal with her, salt suddenly becomes something that people are willing to kill for.

Guest Stars: Kim Hunter, John Doucette, James Best, Myron Healey, Robert Patten, David Pritchard, Ken Drake, John Jay Douglas

Written by: B.W. Sandefur

Directed by: Leon Benson

289. Blood Tie, *February 18, 1968*

The Cartwrights are tricked into hiring Tracy Blaine after Tracy and his accomplice stage a scene allowing him to save Joe's life. Another accomplice, posing as a bounty hunter, claims Tracy is wanted in Arizona. When Ben interferes, the bounty hunter shoots him in the leg. After Hoss and Joe ride off to find the bounty hunter, the men hold Ben hostage and demand the money in the safe. But Tracy has never had any blood ties, and he has grown to like the Cartwrights.

Guest Stars: Robert Drivas, Conlan Carter, Leo Gordon, Peter Leeds

Written by: Arthur Dales

Directed by: Seymour Robbie

290. The Crime of Johnny Mule, *February 25, 1968*

Johnny Mule is on trial for murdering David Loudon. Everyone including Loudon's two sons think it's an open and shut case. Hoss is the only holdout on the jury, even after three days. Johnny breaks jail to avoid a lynching. It won't be easy for Hoss to prove Johnny's innocence after his jailbreak.

Guest Star: Noah Beery

Written by: Joel Murcott

Directed by: Leon Benson

291. The Late Ben Cartwright, *March 3, 1968*

Sam Endicott contributes a lot of money to Judge John Faraday's gubernatorial campaign. Ben refuses to give his necessary endorsement, since he knows Endicott is corrupt. When he promises to nominate the incumbent governor, Endicott hires a gunman to kill Ben.

Guest Stars: Sidney Blackmer, Bert Freed, William Campbell, Simon Scott, George Gaynes, Tyler McVey

Written by: Walter Black

Directed by: Leon Benson

292. Star Crossed, *March 10, 1968*

Candy falls in love with Laura Jean Pollard, a woman obviously down on her luck. He brings her to a boarding house, and persuades Ben to find her a job. The former marshal of Laura's hometown comes to Virginia City looking for her. Laura had killed a man in self-defense, and the marshal told her to run away. Now the marshal is insisting that she marry Joe the wealthy Cartwright instead of Candy the ranch hand, so he can continue to collect blackmail payments.

Guest Stars: Tisha Sterling, William Windom

Written by: Thomas Thompson

Directed by: William F. Claxton

293. Trouble Town, *March 17, 1968*

While in River Bend, Candy meets a saloon girl named Lila, who is obviously in trouble. Candy is determined to help her, and resigns his employment with Ben. Meanwhile, Ben's men get into a few fights in the saloon, and the sheriff of the town charges Ben many times the actual damage value. When Candy discovers the roulette wheel in the saloon is rigged, Candy is imprisoned without bail. Ben finds out the sheriff killed two men who had something in common with Candy. They had also tried to help Lila.

Guest Stars: Robert Wilke, Elizabeth MacRae, Steve Brodie

Written by: David Lang

Directed by: Leon Benson

294. Commitment at Angelus, *April 7, 1968*

While in Angelus, Joe sees his friend, Steve Regan, a miner. Steve tells Joe the miners have gone on strike; the timber supports in the tunnels are rotting away. Joe offers him a day's wages to help him drive horses. Steve is killed when a horse throws him. Joe blames himself, and feels responsible for Steve's widow. She tells Joe that Steve would want him to help the miners - not an easy task.

Guest Stars: Peter Whitney, Marj Dusay, Ken Lynch, Ivan Triesault, Greg Mulleavy, Hal Lynch, Alan Reynolds

Written by: Peter Germano

Directed by: Leon Benson

295. A Dream to Dream, *April 14, 1968*

Hoss goes to Josh Carter's ranch to buy horses. Josh Carter is a drunk, and he treats his wife, Sarah and two children like strangers. Sarah and the children immediately warm up to Hoss. Sarah tells Hoss that Josh was once a loving husband and father. Things changed three years ago when their oldest son, Michael, was killed in a horse accident.

Guest Stars: Steve Ihnat, Julie Harris

Written by: Michael Landon

Directed by: William F. Claxton

Michael Landon frames a shot for "To Die in Darkness", his directorial debut

296. In Defense of Honor, *April 28, 1968*

Ben's favorite horsebreaker, Davey, had been left behind by his Yute tribe after his mother and father were killed. Ben has looked after him since he was five. Even though Davey thinks of himself as white, he still has red skin, which brings him constant torment from a group of bigots. Trouble starts when Davey falls in love with Bright Moon, the daughter of the Yute Chief. She has promised to marry White Wolf, who despises Davey for being neither an Indian nor a white man.

Guest Stars: Lou Antonio, Arnold Moss, Ned Romero, Lane Bradford, Cherie Latimer, Troy Melton, John Lodge, Arthur Peterson

Written by: William Douglas Lansford, Richard Wendley

Directed by: Marc Daniels

297. To Die In Darkness, *May 5, 1968*

John Postley is released from the Nevada State Prison, where he had served a year and a half. Another man had just confessed to the robbery that he was jailed for. Ben's testimony played a key role in the conviction. Postley traps Ben and Candy underground to make them realize the pain that he went through in prison. Michael Landon made his directorial debut with this episode

Guest Star: James Whitmore

Written by: Michael Landon

Directed by: Michael Landon

298. The Bottle Fighter, *May 12, 1968*

Hoss is accused of killing Warren Edwards. Hoss had agreed to sell Edwards 1,000 steer, but Edwards backed out on the deal. Hoss can't remember recent events due to a head injury, and the evidence is clearly against him. Ben rushes to Salt Springs and tries desperately to hire a defense lawyer. All the lawyers know if they want to continue to practice, they can't defend Hoss Cartwright. The only lawyer that Ben can get is Barney Sturgis, once a brilliant Sacramento trial lawyer, now the town drunk.

Guest Star: Albert Dekker

Written by: John Hawkins, Colin Mackenzie, S.H. Barnett

Directed by: Leon Benson

299. The Arrival of Eddie, *May 19, 1968*

Hoss feels responsible for Eddie Makay; he was forced to kill Eddie's father. Despite Eddie's past, Hoss hires him. A rancher, from whom Eddie stole $75 a while back, buys several horses from Ben. When Eddie delivers them, he makes Eddie sign the receipt and leave for San Francisco. The Cartwrights will think Eddie stole the money. He threatens to put Eddie in jail for the $75 theft if he doesn't do as he says.

Guest Star: Michael Vincent

Written by: Ward Hawkins, John M. Chester

Directed by: Marc Daniels

300. The Stronghold, *May 26, 1968*

Joe sells a herd of cattle to the Farrell brothers, but the bank teller who signs the cashier's check is an impostor employed by the Farrell's. When Joe learns the check was a forgery, he and Candy go to the Farrell's ranch in Arizona.

Guest Stars: Michael Witney, Paul Mantee, Lynda Day, James Davidson

Written by: John Hawkins, W.R. Burnett

Directed by: Leon Benson

301. Pride of A Man, *June 2, 1968*

When Joe's friend Abby Pettigrew, the local school-teacher, is injured in a horse accident, Joe fills the unaccustomed role of schoolteacher. He's faced with the challenge of getting the McNabb brothers, Billy and Willy, to go to school. Their father is a hog farmer, and doesn't think his sons need an education.

Guest Star: Morgan Woodward

Written by: Ward Hawkins, Helen B. Hicks

Directed by: William F. Claxton

302. A Severe Case of Matrimony, *July 7, 1968*

The Cartwrights sense trouble when a band of gypsies claim to be stranded with a broken wagon wheel. Ben knows not to trust Encermo, but no one is prepared for the con artistry of Encermo's niece, Rosalita. She runs to the Ponderosa begging for shelter, claiming she is of high Castilian ancestry, and the gypsies have been holding her captive for years. Her mission? To romance a Cartwright into backing her operatic career.

Guest Stars: J. Carrol Naish, Susan Strasberg

Written by: Michael Fessier

Directed by: Lewis Allen

303. Stage Door Johnnies, *July 28, 1968*

Hoss and Joe tangle over Miss Denise, the snobby new chanteuse at the saloon. When her lap dog, Andre, gets lost, Hoss figures that finding the dog is the key to winning Denise's affections. He tells Denise he will offer a reward as big as she wants, and Joe finds it hilarious when she puts an ad in the paper offering $1,000.

Guest Stars: Kathleen Crowley, Walter Brooke, Mike Mazurki

Written by: Alex Sharp

Directed by: William F. Claxton

SEASON 10

304. Different Pines, Same Wind,
September 15, 1968

Lumber tycoon Jason Milburn has been taking advantage of a legal loophole to cut down the forests. The law says if someone doesn't own land in Nevada, he can make improvements on a quarter-section, then file a claim for $200. Milburn's employees file claims, then sell Milburn the land for $1. While attempting to stop him, Joe meets Kerry Pickett. She's lived on a small plot of land for many years, but never filed a claim. It's up to Joe to save Kerry's land.

Guest Stars: Irene Tedrow, John Randolph, Herbert Voland, G.D. Spradlin, George Murdock, John L. Wheeler

Written by: Suzanne Clauser

Directed by: Leon Benson

305. Child, *September 22, 1968*

Hoss is arrested for murder and theft in a remote town. The town's richest man had just been murdered, and the townspeople are less concerned with justice than finding his money. They're convinced that if they threaten Hoss, he'll tell them where he hid the fortune. A few top citizens, including the mayor, form a lynch mob to hang Hoss "part of the way." But Cowboy Child Barnett breaks Hoss out of jail, and the two men form a friendship on the run.

Guest Stars: John Marley, Harry Hickok, Yaphet Kotto, Henry Beckman, Frank DeVol, Robert Ball, Charles Maxwell, Bruce Kirby

Written by: Jack B. Sowards

Directed by: Leon Benson

306. Salute to Yesterday,
September 29, 1968

The Cartwrights and Candy help Captain Harris and his soldiers fight off Mexican gold thieves. The head of the outlaw gang is Candy's childhood friend, and Mrs. Harris is Candy's former wife, Ann. Immediately after their marriage, Ann's father had the marriage annulled. Candy sneaks into the enemy camp to steal supplies to impress Ann. Captain Harris, jealous of Candy, tries also and is captured. We learn about Candy's past - his father was a war hero who died when Candy was seven; his mother died of "loneliness and the frontier life" when Candy was four.

Guest Stars: Pat Conway, Sandra Smith, John Kellogg, Carlos Rivas, Richard Lapp, Troy Melton, Rudy Diaz, Pepe Callahan

Written by: John Hawkins

Directed by: Leon Benson

Dan Blocker returned to Sul Ross in 1966 with Lorne Greene to perform in a production of "The Greatest Glory". Here, they rehearse with Dan's college mentor, Freda Gibson-Powell.

GOLD KEY

BONANZA

10036-806 JUNE

BONANZA

12¢

The Cartwrights discover they're riding living bombs when their mules turn out to be loaded with nitroglycerin!

307. The Real People of Muddy Creek,
October 6, 1968

When Sheriff Walker is murdered, Ben and Joe deliver Luke Harper to the Muddy Creek jail. But when they ask for help from the local residents, everyone leaves town. The Harper brothers are on their way to bust their brother out of jail, and no one is brave enough to fight. That is, no one but Mrs. Walker, the sheriff's widow; Casey Collins, a saloon girl; Haines, an old man; and Simon, his young grandson.

Guest Stars: Joe Don Baker, Clifton James, Jean Hale, Ann Doran, Hal Lynch, Russell Thorson

Written by: Alf Harris

Directed by: Leon Benson

308. The Passing of a King,
October 13, 1968

Poor Mexican settler Mr. Rodriguez is hanged for butchering a Double "R" calf, not a hanging crime. The man responsible is Jeremy, son of ranch owner Claude Roman. Jeremy has declared his physically disabled father incompetent. Claude is helpless against his son.

Guest Stars: Jeremy Slate, Denver Pyle, Diana Muldaur, Dan Tobin, Russ Conway

Written by: B.W. Sandefur

Directed by: Leon Benson

309. The Last Vote,
October 20, 1968

Hoss and Joe bet on the upcoming mayoral election, where the loser pays for the winner's vacation to San Francisco. The two candidates are Titus Simpson and Phineas Burke, two longtime friends who don't care about the election outcome. With a large bet at stake, the two Cartwrights volunteer themselves as campaign managers – Joe for Titus Simpson and Hoss for Phineas Burke.

Guest Stars: Tom Bosley, Wally Cox, Robert Emhardt, Bing Russell, Don Haggerty, Lane Bradford, Bruno Ve Sota

Written by: Robert Vincent Wright

Directed by: Joseph Pevney

310. Catch as Catch Can, *October 27, 1968*

The Cartwrights stop in Tinbucket during a cattle drive. Trouble starts in the saloon, where Candy is accused of cheating at poker. Then, everyone tells Ben how sorry they are that he's bankrupt. Someone drugs Hoss' sasparilla, and Joe is accused of pickpocketing. To round things out, Ben is accused of dealing in stolen hides when the bar-E brand is found on all his skins. The Cartwrights cannot imagine who is orchestrating everything and why.

Written by: David Lang

Directed by: Robert L. Friend

311. Little Girl Lost, *November 3, 1968*

Ben gets an unusual package on the Wells Fargo Express, a tomboy named Samantha. Her mother is Ben's distant relative and she sent Samantha to stay at the Ponderosa until she can leave her saloon job. Ben has his hands full with Samantha. Samantha's father has abandoned them, and her mother wants open a dress shop in Virginia City. All's well until Samantha's paternal grandfather demands custody. He doesn't feel her mother is fit.

Guest Stars: Linda Sue Risk, Antoinette Bower

Written by: Michael Fessier

Directed by: Don Richardson

312. The Survivors, *November 10, 1968*

Alicia Purcell was captured by the Paiutes four years ago and has been the chief warlord's squaw ever since. The Army captures the tribe, which had been raiding towns for years. Alicia wants to live on an Indian reservation. She had a child with the chief, and she knows how half-breeds are treated in white towns. Ben persuades her to stay at the Ponderosa while she reconsiders her decision, but no one will accept her or her child, not even her husband.

Guest Stars: Mariette Hartley, John Carter, Martin Ashe, Harriet Medin

Written by: S.H. Barnett, Colin MacKenzie, John Hawkins

Directed by: Leon Benson

313. The Sound of Drums, *November 17, 1968*

The sound of drums cues big trouble between Ben and neighbor Giorgio Rossi. Despite Ben's warning, Rossi invites a band of Indians to camp on his land, then learns that they think they've been invited to live there.

Guest Stars: Jack Kruschen, Penny Santon, Brioni Farrell, Michael Stefani, Byron Morrow, Joaquin Martinez, Mark Tapscott, Debra Domasin, Pete Hernandez

Written by: William F. Leicester

Directed by: Robert L. Friend

314. Queen High, *December 1, 1968*

Candy and Joe win an ore processing mill in a poker game. Or so they thought. The deed is actually worth only 40 percent of the mill; the other 60 percent is owned by a beautiful woman named Katie Kelly. Joe and Candy love the idea of having Miss Kate for a partner, and spend their evenings trying to win her attention. They spend their days fighting Miles Renfrow. He has orchestrated several "accidents" in the past to preserve his monopoly over the miners.

Guest Stars: Celeste Yarnell, Paul Lambert, Sandor Szabo, Dabney Coleman, Ken Drake, Edward Schaaf

Written by: Michael Fessier

Directed by: Leon Benson

315. Yonder Man, *December 8, 1968*

Joe finds a seemingly harmless old man crossing the Ponderosa. The man bets Joe that he can ride Cochise to the ridge in ten seconds. He does it, but then rides away. Candy catches him and tries to bring him to the sheriff. But Ben recognizes the horse thief as his old friend, Beaudry. Ben and Beaudry were buddies in the Texas-Mexico war, and Beaudry has been drifting ever since. Now, he wants to build himself a spread in Mira Flores, and he needs Ben's investment to start out.

Guest Stars: John Vernon, Melissa Murphy, Rodolfo Acosta, Larry Ward

Written by: Milton S. Gelman

Directed by: Leo Penn

316. Mark of Guilt, *December 15, 1968*

Emo Younger cuts off Hop Sing's pigtail. Hop Sing is devastated, since Chinese belief says the pigtail is necessary to enter heaven. Joe confronts Emo Younger and recovers the pigtail. Later, Emo Younger is found murdered with a 2-by-4. The weapon had been freshly painted, and Joe has paint on his hands. He's arrested for murder, and faces certain hanging. It's up to Hop Sing to return the favor that Joe did for him.

Guest Stars: Dick Foran, Michael Vandever, Alan Bergman, Lou Frizzell, Gordon Dilworth

Written by: Ward Hawkins, Frank Telford

Directed by: Leon Benson

317. A World Full of Cannibals,
December 22, 1968

Ben agrees to hide Charles Ball on the Ponderosa. Ball had committed fraud, and is scheduled to testify against eight former accomplices. The eight men will stop at nothing to ensure Ball doesn't live to testify. Desperate, Charles makes a deal with seven of the men to place all the blame on the eighth.

Guest Star: James Patterson

Written by: Preston Wood

Directed by: Hellstrom Gunner

318. Sweet Annie Laurie, *January 5, 1969*

Hoss finds Laurie Adams hiding in his wagon. She's running from her husband, Kelly. Kelly tricks Laurie into seeing him, and says he will kill Hoss if she doesn't go with him to Mexico. She kills him in self-defense, or so she thinks. Kelly kills Paul Rogers, takes his clothes, and changes his name to Henry Winters. Now that everyone thinks he's dead, he's free to do whatever he wants.

Guest Stars: Joan Van Ark, James Olson, Lawrence Dane, James Jeter

Written by: John Hawkins, Kay Lenard, Jess Carneol, Jackson Gillis

Directed by: Don Richardson

319. My Friend, My Enemy,
January 12, 1969

Candy is charged with murdering John Leggett, and it's up to the Cartwrights to save him. Things couldn't be more difficult: the only witness is an elusive Indian horse thief, the defense will be handled by an unenthusiastic lawyer, and the case will be heard by a man known as the "the hanging judge."

Guest Stars: John Saxon, Woodrow Parfrey, Chick Chandler, Gregory Walcott, Ben Hammer, Raymond Guth, Sunshine Parker, Duane Grey

Written by: Jack B. Sowards and Stanley Roberts

Directed by: Leon Benson

320. Mrs. Wharton and the Lesser Breeds,
January 19, 1969

While on an errand, Candy earns extra money by assisting Mrs. Wharton, a smart-mouthed British matron. When the stagecoach is robbed and Mrs.

Wharton's jewels are stolen, Candy gets more work than he bargained for. Mrs. Wharton insists on going into the lawless town where her stolen jewels are hidden. Candy goes with her, thinking she'll never get out alive. But he learns he can take some lessons from Mrs. Wharton in catching crooks.

Guest Stars: Mildred Natwick, Oren Stevens

Written by: Preston Wood

Directed by: Leon Benson

321. Erin, *January 26, 1969*

Hoss agrees trade beef for wild horses with Chief Red Eagle, after he notices the tribe's best horse catcher, Erin O'Donnell. Erin was born on a ship from Ireland, and was adopted by the Sioux Indians after her mother died. Erin had been thrown from a horse shortly before meeting Hoss, and her shoulder is rapidly becoming infected. Hoss brings her to the Ponderosa to care for her, and soon decides he wants to marry her. But the Cartwrights' neighbor, Mr. Murray, is afraid Erin will attract Indians into the area.

Guest Stars: Mary Fickett, Don Briggs, Michael Keep, Joan Tompkins

Written by: Sandy Summerhays

Directed by: Don Richardson

322. Company of Forgotten Men,
February 2, 1969

A ragged band of Army veterans who have received no pension from the United States government plan to rob the Carson City mint and keep the gold until the government agrees to a pension. Their old buddy, Candy, becomes their unwilling assistant. He must do whatever they say; they're carrying nitroglycerin.

Guest Stars: James Gregory, Charles Maxwell, John Pickard, Ken Lynch, William Bryant

Written by: Kay Lenard and Jess Carneol

Directed by: Leon Benson

323. The Clarion, *February 9, 1969*

Ben meets his old friend, Ruth Manning. Ruth has been the owner and publisher of Gunlock's newspaper, the Clarion, ever since her husband died. Judge Seth Tabor controls everything in Gunlock except the Clarion, and will stop at nothing to control that too. After several scare tactics, Ruth agrees to sell the

Clarion to Tabor. Ben offers to handle the sale and, without Ruth's knowledge, buys the Clarion himself.

Guest Stars: Phyllis Thaxter, Simon Oakland, William Jordan, Hamilton Camp, Philip Kennally, Ken Mayer, Connie Sawyer, James Jeter, Arthur Peterson, Ed McCready

Written by: John Hawkins and Frank Chase

Directed by: Lewis Allen

324. The Lady and the Mountain Lion, *February 23, 1969*

"The Magnificent Malcolm", a traveling magician comes to town, and Hoss and Joe both fall in love with his daughter. Trouble is, they don't realize the magician really has twin daughters, Janet and Janice (both called "Jan"). One spends her time reciting poetry, the other sinking billiard balls at the pool hall.

Guest Stars: Richard Haydn, Michael Keep

Written by: Larry Markes

Directed by: Joseph Pevney

325. Five Candles, *March 2, 1969*

A mine explosion triggers the collapse of the Virginia City courthouse, leaving Ben trapped in the basement with Bristol Toby, an Irish miner on trial for murder; Callie, the courthouse clerk; Jonathan Pike, her fiance and the chief witness against the miner; and a critically injured lawman.

Guest Stars: Scott Thomas, Don Knight

Written by: Ken Trevey

Directed by: Lewis Allen

326. The Wish, *March 9, 1969*

While on a two-month vacation, Hoss befriends a black boy who constantly wishes his father were white. When he brings the boy home, he finds his family near poverty. Their farm had been hit by a drought, and neither the father, an ex-slave, or the older brother, can find work because of their race.

Guest Stars: Ossie Davis, George Spell

Written by: Michael Landon

Directed by: Michael Landon

327. The Deserter, *March 16, 1969*

Candy befriends Sam Bellis, an Army sergeant charged with desertion and murder. He is accused of running away during an Indian war. Bellis insists he was justified; the Indians had superior firepower. When Army officials don't believe that the Indians have high-powered rifles, Candy, Bellis, and Bellis' wife Nanata look for the source of those rifles.

Guest Stars: Ford Rainey, Ellen Davalos

Written by: B.W. Sandefur, John Dunkel

Directed by: Leon Benson

328. Emily, *March 23, 1969*

Joe sees his ex-fiancee, Emily Anderson, in Virginia City. Emily and Joe are still in love with each other, but Emily "forgets" to tell Joe that she's now married to Deputy Marshal Wade McPhail. That's just the beginning of Emily's lies, which eventually get Joe shot and nearly framed for robbery and murder.

Guest Stars: Beth Brickell, Ron Hayes

Written by: Preston Wood, Elliott Gilbert

Directed by: Leon Benson

329. The Running Man, *March 30, 1969*

Candy gets a letter from an old girlfriend, Barbara Parker, begging for his help. Several homesteaders in Butlerville have been burned out of their homes. Now Butler and his men are guilty of murder; a woman and child died in one of the fires. Barbara's husband, Jess, is the only witness.

Guest Stars: Robert Pine, Will Geer

Written by: John and Ward Hawkins

Directed by: Leon Benson

330. The Unwanted, *April 6, 1969*

Ben gets a visit from his old friend Marshal Luke Mansfield and his daughter, Lorrie. Luke is hunting escaped convict Billy Miller, who had put a bullet in his leg. Ben has a ranch hand named Rick Miller, who finally admits he's Billy's cousin. He says Billy died immediately after escaping. The marshal doesn't believe him, and he, Joe and Candy look for the grave. While they're gone, Lorrie and Rick fall in love.

Guest Stars: Bonnie Bedelia, Charles McGraw, Michael Vincent

Written by: Thomas Thompson and Suzanne Clauser

Directed by: Herschel Daugherty

331. Speak No Evil, *April 20, 1969*

When 14-year-old Coley's father dies and leaves him a gold mine, Ben and Hoss are drawn into the middle of a custody battle. Coley's long lost mother and sister return after four years and try to win Coley back, but Coley's greedy uncle Clayborne has his sights squarely planted on that gold mine.

Guest Stars: Patricia Smith, Kevin Burchett, Dana Elcar

Written by: B.W. Sandefur, Norman Katkov

Directed by: Leon Benson

332. The Fence, *April 27, 1969*

Ben and Hoss visit their friend Sam Masters and his daughter, Ellen, and learn they're constantly on the run. Soon, soldiers start shooting at Sam's house, demanding his surrender. Sam's real name is Thomas Andrews. During the Civil War, he ran a prison camp for captured Union soldiers. Five hundred men died from starvation and disease, and now Colonel Jim Hudson and his men have come to take revenge.

Guest Stars: J.D. Cameron, John Anderson, Larry Linville, Charles Dierkop, Gary Walberg, Frank Webb, Verna Bloom, Patrick Hawkey

Written by: Ward Hawkins, Milton S. Gelman, Alf Harris

Directed by: Lewis Allen

333. A Ride in the Sun, *May 11, 1969*

Traveling con artists Tobias and April Horn rob the Virginia City bank and shoot Ben. They plan to elude the posse by crossing the desert; their accomplice has hidden several water caches. Joe chases them across the desert, without realizing they poisoned the water holes with arsenic.

Guest Stars: Robert Hogan, Anthony Zerbe, Marj Dusay, Jack Collins

Written by: John Hawkins, Peter Germano

Directed by: Leon Benson

Season 11

334. Another Windmill to Go,
September 14, 1969

Hoss and Candy find the eccentric Don Q. Hoat "rowing" a boat on wheels across dry land. Ben had been leasing that grazing land from the government for $1,200 a year, and often worries about losing the lease. He doesn't feel threatened by Hoat until Hoat files a claim on the land. An obscure law, called the Federal Swamp and Marsh Act says that a man can claim for $1.50 an acre whatever he can cross in a rowboat from sunup to sundown.

Guest Stars: *Laurence Naismith, Jill Townsend*

Written by: *Palmer Thompson*

Directed by: *James B. Clark*

335. The Witness, *September 21, 1969*

During a stagecoach robbery, one man is murdered and another is gravely wounded. That leaves no witnesses, until Jenny Winters says she saw the Logan brothers rob the stage and shoot the two men. The Logan brothers are known for never leaving any witnesses alive, so Ben offers Jenny refuge on the Ponderosa until they are caught.

Guest Stars: *Stefan Gierasch, Melissa Murphy*

Written by: *Joel Murcott*

Directed by: *Don Richardson*

336. The Silence At Stillwater,
September 28, 1969

Candy is mysteriously jailed in Stillwater by the acting sheriff. Candy had been carrying a lot of money to purchase horses, which the sheriff uses as evidence against him. The Cartwrights go to Stillwater to meet Candy, but the sheriff won't tell them that Candy is in jail. He says he doesn't want any "outside interference". Candy is charged with murder and robbery, the son of a victim is a positive eyewitness, and the sheriff will not let him prepare a defense.

Guest Stars: *Pat Hingle, Strother Martin*

Written by: *Preston Wood*

Directed by: *Josef Leytes*

337. A Lawman's Lot Is Not A Happy One,
October 5, 1969

Hoss is made temporary sheriff after he inadvertently beats up the deputy who had come to fill in for Roy. A beautiful woman named Sissy Somers arrives on the stage to marry Haram Peabody, the stage office attendant. They had been writing letters, but they never met. Peabody panics when he sees Sissy; he had told her that he's tall, rich and handsome. He plans on avoiding her by landing himself in jail. He does everything imaginable to get arrested, but Hoss still refuses to put him in jail. Meanwhile, Mr. Forbes and his butler, Fairfax, come to Virginia City to build a resort hotel. The town falls in love with Forbes, and is eager to invest. Hoss finds a warrant for the arrest of a 200+ pound businessman, and Forbes fits that description. Hoss arrests him, and the town is furious. How could he jail the wonderful Mr. Forbes and not the criminal Haram Peabody?

Guest Stars: *Tom Bosley*

Written by: *Robert Vincent Wright*

Directed by: *Don Richardson*

338. Anatomy of a Lynching,
October 12, 1969

Virginia City is in an uproar after Will Griner is acquitted of murder. The townspeople are sure that witnesses were silenced, and talk of lynching is getting louder. Although Ben feels Griner is guilty, he can't allow a lynching. Roy Coffee puts Griner in jail for his own protection. While trying to avert a lynching, Ben tries to reopen the case by proving that witnesses were silenced.

Guest Stars: *Guy Stockwell, Tyler McVey*

Written by: *Preston Wood*

Directed by: *William Wiard*

339. To Stop A War, *October 19, 1969*

The local cattle ranches are plagued by rustlers, so the Cattlemen's Association decides to hire a range detective. Joe suggests ex-marshal Dan Logan. Against Ben's wishes, Frank Slader offers Logan $300 for each rustler brought in dead or alive.

Guest Stars: *Steve Forrest, Miriam Colon, Warren Kemmerling, Bing Russell, Richard Bull, Chuck Bail, John Tracy, Ollie O'Toole, Alan Vint*

Written by: *Carey Wilbur*

Directed by: *Leon Benson*

340. The Medal, *October 26, 1969*

Ben befriends Matthew Rush, a Congressional Medal of Honor recipient, who he finds drunk in the saloon. Recognizing his wartime achievements, Ben offers him shelter and a job at the Ponderosa. He agrees to stay for awhile, but Ben's friend Seth Nagel and his son, Walt, are determined to run him out of town or kill him. The Nagel's were Southerners, and their town was burned by Union soldiers.

Guest Stars: *Dean Stockwell, Harry Townes, Susan Howard, Charles Briles, Remo Pisani, John Beck, Sundown Spencer, James Rawley, E.J. Schuster*

Written by: *Frank Chase*

Directed by: *Lewis Allen*

341. The Stalker, *November 2, 1969*

Candy witnesses a robbery and shoots the robber in self defense. He recognizes the outlaw as James Campbell, who used to do some farming on the Ponderosa. The inquest absolves Candy, but he feels guilty after seeing Campbell's widow, Lisa, and their young son. He volunteers to work on Lisa's farm, and a romance begins to blossom. Shortly after the shooting, Lisa had written a letter to her brother-in-law, Jake asking him to kill Candy. Now she has changed her mind, but Jake has not.

Guest Stars: *Charlotte Stewart, Lloyd Battista, John Perak*

Written by: *D.C. Fontana*

Directed by: *Robert L. Friend*

342. Meena, *November 16, 1969*

Joe and Candy are picking up supplies when they spot Meena Calhoun. They race to follow her to the remote gold mine where she lives with her father. Joe is stopped along the way by a trio of bumbling outlaws and soon escapes, without his horse. He finds the Calhoun residence, but Luke Calhoun refuses to lend him a horse. At that moment, Meena it's time to get married, and Joe just happens to be there.

Guest Stars: *Ann Prentiss, Victor French, Dub Taylor, Robert Donner*

Written by: *Jack B. Sowards*

Directed by: *Herschel Daugherty*

343. A Darker Shadow, *November 23, 1969*

Wade Turner's life is shaping up wonderfully. He just got a promotion and he and Sarah are making wedding plans. Suddenly, he tells Sarah they can't get married, and gives no explanation. He leaves town after stealing $5,000 from the bank's cash supply. The doctor in Willow Bend tells him he has a brain tumor, and he will go blind if it is not removed.

Guest Stars: *Gregory Walcott*

Written by: *John Hawkins, Jonathan Knopf, B.W. Sandefur*

Directed by: *Don Richardson*

344. Dead Wrong, *December 7, 1969*

Hoss and Candy accidentally spill a bag of money from a cattle sale. Salty Hubbard, the tall-tale teller of Sunville is convinced that Hoss is the notorious bank robber "Big Jack". Poor Hoss can't figure out why the whole town is afraid of him. He tries to take care of some banking, but he's told the bank is closed for "Good Tuesday". Meanwhile, the real Big Jack can't figure out why his planned bank heist is going so smoothly.

Guest Stars: *Mike Mazurki, Robert Sorrells*

Written by: *Michael Landon*

Directed by: *Michael Landon*

345. Old Friends, *December 14, 1969*

Jess Waddell, Charlie Sheppard and Ben were close friends 25 years ago. Now they're having a strange and sad reunion. Charlie is a wanted outlaw and Jess is a bounty hunter on his trail. It's up to Ben to calm Jess' itchy trigger finger since Charlie has taken Hoss prisoner.

Guest Stars: *Robert J. Wilke, Morgan Woodward*

Written by: *Barney Slater*

Directed by: *Leon Benson*

346. Abner Willoughby's Return, *December 21, 1969*

Abner Willoughby had buried a cache of gold, and tries to steal Joe's horse to retrieve it. Joe finds Abner amusing and goes with him. When they get there, they find that a town has sprung up on the once-empty land. Abner's gold is buried under a henhouse belonging to a widow, her young son and her gun-crazy mother.

Guest Stars: John Astin, Emmaline Henry

Written by: Jack B. Sowards, Leslie McFarlane

Directed by:

347. It's A Small World, *January 4, 1970*

No one wants to hire George, a midget who used to work for the circus. When the banker won't hire him, George robs the bank. He's caught immediately and returns the money. The banker, however, is determined to press charges. That is, until George is the only one who can save the banker's daughter after she falls down a well.

Guest Stars: Michael Dunn, Edward Binns, Bing Russell, Angela Clark

Written by: Michael Landon

Directed by: Michael Landon

348. Danger Road, *January 11, 1970*

The Campbell Freight Company has a monopoly and charges everyone exorbitant rates. Candy meets Gunny Riley, a drifter who hauls freight for a living. Ben and Gunny were soldiers together in the Mexican War, and Gunny's beard covers the brand of "D" for deserter. Ben decides to give Gunny a job mostly for his wife's sake, and because he despises Campbell Freight. After realizing Gunny's a man capable of loyalty, Ben prepares him for a race against Campbell for a lucrative government contract.

Guest Stars: Robert Lansing, Anna Novarro, William Sylvester

Written by: Milton S. Gelman, Brian McKay

Directed by: William F. Claxton

349. The Big Jackpot, *January 18, 1970*

Joe and Hoss give Candy the worst job on the Ponderosa, cleaning water holes. Candy has the last laugh when he finds out he's inherited a fortune. When word gets around, society people surround him, offering to make deals and marry off their daughters. He takes a liking to a land promoter, who makes him Vice President of the company and gives him a large office. But the promoter is promising beautiful, fertile land and selling nothing but desert wasteland.

Guest Stars: Walter Brooke, Robert F. Simon, Alan Caillou

Written by: John Hawkins

Directed by: Herschel Daugherty

350. The Trouble With Amy, *January 25, 1970*

Amy Wilder is a sharp-tongued widow who combats her loneliness by opening her heart and home to all wild animals, even a skunk named Harriet. When a land developer offers her a generous sum for some unused land, she refuses to sell. The deer need that land to graze and to walk down to the water. The land baron tries to have Amy declared senile and put in an institution.

Guest Stars: Jo Van Fleet, John Crawford, Donald Moffatt

Written by: Jack Miller, John Hawkins

Directed by: Leon Benson

351. The Lady and the Mark, *February 1, 1970*

Former Ponderosa hand Chris Keller has found a gold strike worth $67,000 so the Cartwrights are puzzled when he comes back seeking work. Con men everywhere have been trying to steal his money, so he has decided to return as a cowhand to escape. Chris rescues Charity McGill from a runaway horse and buggy. Chris asks Charity to marry him, but tragedy has struck Charity's family. Her father writes to her saying if he doesn't get $65,000 he will lose his gold mine.

Guest Stars: Elaine Giftos, James Westerfield, Christopher Connelly

Written by: Preston Wood

Directed by: Leon Benson

352. Is There Any Man Here, *February 8, 1970*

Jennifer Carlisle has grown into an independent woman and engineer. She comes to Virginia City ostensibly to check on a project. Ben soon learns the real reason. She left her groom, an influential banker, at the altar in San Francisco. Jennifer is the same age as Ben's sons, but she's made up her mind to marry Ben. But her jilted groom comes to Virginia City to take her back, and will ruin Ben if she doesn't go with him.

Guest Stars: John Liam, Mariette Hartley, Burr DeBenning

Written by: B.W. Sandefur

Directed by: Don Richardson

353. The Law and Billy Burgess, *February 15, 1970*

When Billy Burgess is forced to attend the new Ponderosa school, he's so angry that he threatens to kill the schoolmaster. When the schoolmaster is murdered several days later, Billy becomes the prime suspect. Matilda Curtis, a wealthy widow, wants Billy to be sentenced to a judge's custody without a trial. This will protect him from certain hanging. Ben, however, wants Billy's innocence proven in court, and insists on a trial.

Guest Stars: Mercedes McCambridge, Les Tremayne, David Cassidy

Written by: Stanley Roberts

Directed by: William F. Claxton

354. Long Way to Ogden, *February 22, 1970*

The winter is coming, and cattlemen are preparing to drive their herds to Ogden and put them on a railroad to Chicago. The price of beef has gone up drastically, and everyone is looking forward a great. But, Emmett J. Whitney, a Chicago meat packer, buys all the cattle car options and offers everyone the insulting price of $3.00 a head for their cattle. He says he will lower his offer by $1.00 each day.

Guest Stars: Kathleen Freeman, Walter Barnes

Written by: Joel Murcott

Directed by: Lewis Allen

355. Return Engagement, *March 1, 1970*

Lotta Crabtree makes a return appearance in Virginia City. At a party at the Ponderosa, her leading man becomes jealous of Hoss. In the final scene of the performance, Lotta's character is supposed to shoot the leading man's character. During the curtain call, we find out there were real bullets in the gun. Hoss is arrested for the murder when the sheriff finds a handful of blanks in his saddlebag.

Guest Stars: Joyce Bulifant, Sally Kellerman

Written by: Stanley Roberts

Directed by: Don Richardson

356. The Gold Mine, *March 8, 1970*

The Cartwrights befriend a Mexican boy who was sold into virtual slavery by his father, and they help him claim the gold strike that is rightfully his, that his two abusive masters are trying to steal.

Guest Stars: Tony De Costa, Bruce Dern

Written by: Robert Buckner, Preston Wood

Directed by: Leon Benson

357. Decision at Los Robles,
March 22, 1970

Ben and Joe stop in Los Robles. Ben sees John Walker bullying a waitress, and comes to her defense. Walker shoots Ben in the back, and Ben kills Walker before he falls unconscious. Los Robles had always been ruled by John Walker and his son, Jed. Jed tells Joe if he doesn't hand Ben over in 24 hours, he will kill one citizen every hour. When Joe asks the citizens for help, he finds a town full of cowards. The biggest coward of all is the doctor. He purposely left the bullet in Ben's back, hoping he'd die within 24 hours.

Guest Stars: William H. Bassett, Joe De Santis, Ted Cassidy

Written by: Michael Landon

Directed by: Michael Landon

358. Caution, Easter Bunny Crossing,
March 29, 1970

Four bumbling outlaws try to rob the Wells Fargo wagon, with some hilarious results, and Hoss dresses up as as the world's biggest Easter bunny to entertain children at a Quaker orphanage.

Guest Stars: Marc Lawrence, Len Lesser

Written by: Larry Markes

Directed by: Bruce Bilson

359. The Horse Traders, *April 5, 1970*

Meena Calhoun is engaged to Virgil, who, with his two brothers, are freeloading off Luke Calhoun's fortune. Finally Luke tells them: no jobs, no wedding. Virgil convinces Luke to become partners in the livery stable business, with Virgil's two brothers as employees. Meanwhile, Hoss and Joe try to make some fast money by selling horses to the livery stable. The two stables are bidding against each other and driving the price up. But the Cartwrights find out that Luke and Virgil have bought both stables and now have complete control over prices, both buying and selling.

Guest Stars: Dub Taylor, Ann Prentiss, Victor French, Lou Frizzell

Written by: Jack B. Sowards

Directed by: Herschel Daugherty

360. What Are Pardners For?,
April 12, 1970

Hoss runs across two bumbling, wanna-be bank robbers, and is arrested for complicity in a bank robbery. When he tries to get everything straightened out, the two incompetent outlaws call him "pardner," getting him into deeper and deeper trouble.

Guest Stars: Slim Pickens, Dabbs Greer, John Beck, Richard Evans

Written by: Jack B. Sowards

Directed by: William F. Claxton

361. A Matter of Circumstance,
April 19, 1970

Ben, Hoss and Candy leave for a cattle drive, but Joe must stay behind to wait for a chuck wagon cook. Shortly after they leave, a thunder and lightening storm hits. One of the horses is spooked, and Joe is trampled. His left arm and left leg are broken, and he's bleeding badly. All alone, he must fight to remain conscious and treat his injuries.

Guest Stars: Ted Gehring, Vincent Van Patten

Written by: B.W. Sandefur

Directed by: William F. Claxton

SEASON 12

362. The Night Virginia City Died,
September 13, 1970

Virginia City is plagued by an arsonist, Clem's fiancee, Janie. Janie has had a compulsion with fire ever since seeing her abusive stepfather burn to death.

Guest Stars: Angel Tompkins, Bing Russell, Phil Brown, Edith Atwater

Written by: John Hawkins

Directed by: William Wiard

363. A Matter of Faith, *September 20, 1970*

This episode marks the first appearance of Jamie (Mitch Vogel), who demonstrates to skeptical townspeople his late father's rainmaking techniques.

Guest Stars: Lou Frizzell, Bruce Gordon

Written by: Jack B. Sowards, John Hawkins, D.C. Fontana

Directed by: William Wiard

364. The Weary Willies,
September 27, 1970

The Ponderosa becomes home for the Weary Willies, post-Civil War drifters, much to the anger of the Virginia City folk. When Angie, an aristocrat's daughter, becomes friendly with Billy, the Weary Willies' leader, her father and boyfriend are furious. Angie is attacked, and Billy faces trial for attempted murder.

Guest Stars: Richard Thomas, Lee Purcell, Lonny Chapman, Elisha Cook

Written by: Robert Pirosh

Directed by: Leo Penn

365. The Wagon, *October 5, 1970*

While on his way home, Hoss is captured and put aboard a wagon bound for territorial prison. The real prisoner has escaped, and the wagon master, Price Buchanan, gets paid for each prisoner he brings in. He also plans on running for office, and an escaped prisoner would not bode well on his record.

Guest Stars: Denver Pyle, Salome Jens, George Murdock

Written by: Ken Pettus

Directed by: James Neilson

366. The Power of Life and Death,
October 11, 1970

Fugitive killer Davis is stranded at a water hole with a badly wounded Ben, while Joe, alone and on foot, strikes across the desert in search of help.

Guest Stars: Rupert Crosse, Lou Frizzell

Written by: Joel Murcott

Directed by: Leo Penn

367. Gideon, the Good, *October 18, 1970*

Joe sees a woman kill a man, but the woman escapes. He reports the crime to Sheriff Gideon Yates; they find a handkerchief with an embroidered "L", and Yates knows the killer is his wife, Lydia. She married him before she got a legal divorce, and she killed her first husband to silence him. When Joe refuses to leave quietly, Gideon orders a manhunt against him.

Guest Stars: Richard Kiley, Terry Moore, A. Martinez, Carmen Zapata

Written by:

Directed by:

368. The Trouble With Trouble,
October 25, 1970

Hoss takes over as temporary sheriff of Trouble, a well-named community that thrives on rowdyism, frustrating Hoss's efforts to bring about law and order.

Guest Stars: Gene Evans, E.J. Andre, G.D. Spradlin

Written by: Jack B. Sowards

Directed by: Herschel Daugherty

369. Thorton's Account, *November 1, 1970*

Ben is injured when his horse throws him down a hill. Joe searches for a wagon and a team to pull him up, but no one is willing to help. They fear that a land baron will take over their ranches, and they must stand by to defend their land at all times.

Guest Stars: Gregory Walcot, Carl Reindel, Heather Menzies, Scott Walker

Written by: Preston Wood

Directed by: William F. Claxton

370. The Love Child, *November 8, 1970*

Etta has been diagnosed with terminal leukemia. She brings her young son, Scott, west to his grandparents. Etta's mother is thrilled, but her father refuses to have them in his house. Scott was conceived when Etta had an affair with a married man, and she ran away to St. Louis seven years before to have her baby.

Guest Stars: Carol Lawson, Will Geer, Josephine Hutchinson

Written by: Michael Landon

Directed by: Michael Landon

371. El Jefe, *November 15, 1970*

The Cartwrights help Ramon Cardenas, who is charged with murder. Ramon killed one of Owen Driscoll's men in self defense. Driscoll Mining Company wanted to buy Ramon's land, and the land of other Mexicans, for 50 cents an acre. When he refused Owen Driscoll tried to burn him out.

Guest Stars: Rodolfo Acosta, Warren Stevens, Jaime Sanchez

Written by: Ken Pettus, Dick McDonagh

Directed by: William F. Claxton

372. The Luck of Pepper Shannon, *November 22, 1970*

Pepper Shannon, a dime-store hero and a wanted man, asks Jamie to "capture" him and bring him to the Virginia City jail to avoid the men chasing him. Jamie learns more about his comic hero than he cares to know when he finds out about Pepper's land scheme.

Guest Stars: Neville Brand, Walter Brooke, Dan Tobin

Written by: John Hawkins, George Schenck, William Marks

Directed by: Nick Webster

373. The Impostors, *December 13, 1970*

Hoss and Joe go to Pineville to look for Joe Bruter. Bruter's son, Randy, Bud York and Gabe Leroy stole

$51,000 from Hoss. Hoss and Joe pretend to be Bud York and Gabe Leroy to collect at least 2/3 of the money. Randy Bruter, the only person who can identify them, is safely tucked away in the Virginia City jail. But the Bruters are most uncooperative.

Guest Stars: Strother Martin, Anthony Colti, Anthony James

Written by: Robert Vincent Wright

Directed by: Lewis Allen

374. Honest John, *December 20, 1970*

Jamie befriends an old wanderer named John and his black crow, and learns a lot about trust.

Guest Star: Jack Elam

Written by:

Directed by:

375. For A Young Lady, *December 27, 1970*

The Cartwrights help a young girl who was put in the care of evil relatives after her grandfather died. Her grandfather mined for gold on the Ponderosa, and Ben let him keep 10% of what he found. Her new caretakers think she owns the mine outright, and they see her as a fast ticket to a gold strike.

Guest Stars: Jewel Blanch, Paul Fix, Madeleine Sherwood

Written by: B.W. Sandefur

Directed by: Don Richardson

376. A Single Pilgrim, *January 3, 1971*

Hoss is accidentally shot by a man who mistakes him for a deer. He brings him back to his house where he lives with his wife and father. His father fears the law, and thinks they will be much better off if Hoss dies. The wife cares for Hoss despite her father-in-law's protests, but her husband can't stand up to his father.

Guest Stars: Beth Brickell, Jeff Corey, John Schuck

Written by: Suzanne Clauser

Directed by: William Wiard

377. The Gold Plated Rifle, *January 10, 1971*

Jamie is picked on by a group of bullies. To prove himself, he tells them he owns a gold-plated rifle, and shows them Ben's most treasured possession. He accidentally breaks it, and Ben punishes him. Tired of authority, Jamie runs away.

Guest Stars: none

Written by: Preston Wood

Directed by: Joseph Pevney

378. Top Hand, *January 17, 1971*

Ben agrees to do a cattle drive with Weatherby, providing his foreman will be trail boss. Weatherby agrees, without knowing that Ben's foreman is Jim Kelly. Kelly used to work for Weatherby before he served time for murder.

Guest Stars: Ben Johnson, Roger Davis

Written by: John Hawkins, Arthur Heinemann

Directed by: William F. Claxton

379. A Deck of Aces, *January 31, 1971*

Bradley Meredith, Ben's exact lookalike, takes advantage of the resemblance to collect money from selling part of the Ponderosa to the railroad. Lorne Greene does an excellent job on the dual role.

Guest Stars: Alan Oppenheimer, Linda Gaye Scott, Charles Dierkop

Written by: Stanley Roberts

Directed by: Lewis Allen

380. The Desperado, *February 7, 1971*

Hoss is held captive by a black couple accused of murder and hiding out from the law.

Guest Stars: Lou Gossett, Marlene Clark, Ramon Bieri

Written by: George Lovell Hayes

Directed by: Phillip Leacock

381. The Reluctant American, *February 14, 1971*

A ranch near the Ponderosa is plagued by rustlers. The owner, who lives in England, sends his assistant and his pregnant wife to rescue the failing ranch.

Guest Stars: Daniel Massey, Jill Haworth, J. Pat O'Malley, Daniel Kemp

Written by: Stanley Roberts

Directed by: Phillip Leacock

382. Shadow of a Hero, *February 21, 1971*

Ben's friend, a heroic general, runs for governor of Nevada. He stands to win easily, until a muckraking reporter comes to town accusing him of murder. The general denies it, admitting he did shoot a couple of Indian horse thieves in self-defense. Joe goes with the reporter to prove that the Indians didn't steal the horses, and the general shot them out of racial hatred.

Guest Stars: Laurence Luckinbill, John Randolph, Linda Watkins

Written by: John Hawkins, B.W. Sandefur, Mel Goldberg

Directed by: Leo Penn

383. The Silent Killer, *February 28, 1971*

Dr. Woodtree had come to Virginia City to start a hospital. Fearing he wouldn't be taken seriously, he claimed he went to Harvard. Doc Martin had him arrested for fraud. But Doc Martin has bigger problems – a deadly flu epidemic has swept the Ponderosa.

Guest Stars: Meg Foster, Harry Holcombe, Louise Latham

Written by: John Hawkins, Edward DeBlasio

Directed by: Leo Penn

384. Terror at 2:00, *March 7, 1971*

Three men arrive in Virginia City posing as photographers covering a treaty signing between the Army and the Paiutes. Their camera equipment hides a Gatling gun. They plan to execute every citizen on the street at 2:00. Their leader, Mr. Ganns, wants to start an Indian war, hoping that all redmen will be exterminated.

Guest Stars: Steve Ihnat, Dabbs Greer, Byron Mabe

Written by: Michael Landon

Directed by: Michael Landon

385. The Stillness Within, *March 14, 1971*

Joe is blinded when a cat knocks over a bottle of nitroglycerin. Feeling useless, he wallows in self-pity. Ben hires Ellen Dobbs from the Institute for the Blind, and is shocked to see that Miss Dobbs herself is blind. Ellen forbids Ben from telling Joe; if he doesn't know, he'll stop believing that blind people are useless.

Guest Stars: Jo Van Fleet, Harry Holcombe, Jeanine Brown

Written by: Suzanne Clauser

Directed by: Michael Landon

386. A Time to Die, *March 21, 1971*

Ben's friend, April Christopher, is bitten by a wolf that's suspected to be rabid. The wolf is tracked down and killed, and its carcass is sent to San Francisco for analysis. The Cartwrights and April wait for the results, but April shows symptoms of rabies even before the results come back.

Guest Stars: Vera Miles, Henry Beckman, Melissa Newman

Written by: Don Ingalls

Directed by: Philip Leacock

387. Winter Kill, *March 28, 1971*

The Ponderosa and other ranches suffer cattle losses from a rough winter. Ben's one Montana steer thrives. When Howie, a neighboring ranch foreman, accidentally shoots the steer, Quarry the ranch owner threatens to put him in prison unless he tells Ben that he saw the steer die in the winter kill. Then the bank would not loan the ranchers the money for a Montana herd, and Quarry can buy out all of the starving ranchers.

Guest Stars: Glenn Corbett, Clifton James, Sheilah Wells

Written by: John Hawkins, Robert Pirosh, Jack Rummler

Directed by: William Wiard

388. Kingdom of Fear, *April 11, 1971*

Ben, Hoss, Joe, Candy and Billy the ranch hand are arrested for trespassing. When Billy protests, he is killed in cold blood. The Cartwrights and Candy are then taken to a prison camp where the sheriff, judge and jury are the same person, known simply as "the judge." He sentences them to six months of hard labor. The judge does this to get slave labor for his gold mine, and no one ever gets out alive.

Guest Stars: Alfred Ryder, Richard Mulligan, Luke Askew

Written by: Michael Landon

Directed by: Michael Landon

389. An Earthquake Called Callahan, *April 11, 1971*

Dusty Rhoades lands in jail, and the only witness who can prove his innocence is a wrestler named Callahan. When he refuses to get involved, Joe beats him in every match and drives him broke. When the law raids the illegal matches, both Joe and Callahan are arrested, and Joe is shocked to see Dusty bail them out. He was released from jail immediately, so Joe suffered through all that for nothing. Callahan's female sideshow act is quite amusing, whenever she sees the color red, she charges forward like a raging bull.

Guest Stars: Victor French, Sandy Duncan, Lou Frizzell, Dub Taylor

Written by: Preston Wood

Directed by: Herschel Daugherty

Season 13

390. The Grand Swing, *September 19, 1971*

When Jamie takes a dangerous shortcut, he loses control of the horses and totals the wagon. Ben tells him to pack for "the grand swing", Ben's periodic trip around the the Ponderosa. While on their journey, they're faced with a sick Indian chief, unwelcome miners, rustlers, and a ranch-hand's marital crisis. Ben wants to teach Jamie about adult responsibility.

Guest Stars: Ralph Moody, Charlotte Stewart, Med Flory, Ted Gehring

Written by: Ward & John Hawkins, William Koenig

Directed by: William F. Claxton

391. Fallen Woman, *September 26, 1971*

Hoss's testimony gets Conway five years in prison. Conway's drunken wife gives her son, Petey, to Hoss. She thinks Petey is Hoss' responsibility, since he convicted his father. Everyone agrees that she is an unfit mother, and that Hoss should adopt Petey. That is, everyone except Hoss.

Guest Stars: Susan Tyrell, Arthur O'Connell, Ford Rainey

Written by: Ward Hawkins

Directed by: Lewis Allen

392. Bushwhacked, *October 3, 1971*

When Joe is shot, a local family takes him in and gets a doctor. The doctor removes a bullet from Joe's leg, but fears removing the one from his back can kill him. The bullet in his back is causing a serious infection. In his delirium, he has nightmares of teepees and wagon wheels, which give a clue to the attacker.

Guest Stars: Richard O'Brien, Peggy McCay, David Huddleston

Written by: Preston Wood

Directed by: William Wiard

393. Rock-A-Bye Hoss, *October 10, 1971*

Hoss gets roped into judging a beautiful baby contest. The mothers will stop at nothing to ensure victory, including bribes, blackmail and threats. One mother threatens to expose a woman who had her child out of wedlock. She had claimed the baby was her late sister's child.

Guest Stars: Edward Andrews, Patricia Harty, Ellen Moss

Written by: Preston Wood, Robert Vincent Wright

Directed by:

394. The Prisoners, *October 17, 1971*

Joe is forced to take an escaped prisoner to jail alone; no easy task considering the prisoner's friend is on the loose and ready to help. Two naive Mexican children also take his side against Joe.

Guest Stars: Michael Witney, Morgan Woodward, Manuel Padilla

Written by: Arthur Heinemann

Directed by: William F. Claxton

395. Cassie, *October 24, 1971*

After Hoss buys a great stallion from Mr. O'Casey, he learns his scheme. O'Casey sells Prince Omar to the highest bidder, and then bets that his other horse, Captain, can out-run Prince Omar. The winner keeps both horses. His daughter, Cassie, rides Captain; the horse cannot lose carrying such a light weight.

Guest Stars: Lisa Gerritsen, Diane Baker, Jack Cassidy

Written by: True Boardman

Directed by: Herschel Daugherty

396. Don't Cry, My Son, *October 31, 1971*

Mark, a young doctor and his wife, Ruth, are expecting their first child in two weeks. They're on their way home when they are stopped by a frantic Mr. Johnson. Mrs. Johnson has gone into labor sooner than expected. While Mark is at the Johnson house delivering their baby, Ruth loses her own baby. Mark steals the Johnson baby, believing it is his.

Guest Stars: Richard Mulligan, Diana Shalet, Dan Ferrone

Written by: Michael Landon

Directed by: Michael Landon

397. Face of Fear, *November 14, 1971*

Jamie's friend witnesses Mr. Trunkett's murder and sees the killer steal Trunkett's identification. Mr. Trunkett was due to inherit a fortune. Jamie's friend, however, is afraid of her father, and refuses to come forward. Ben hires the killer for temporary work after "Mr. Trunkett" says he needs money until the inheritance comes through.

Guest Stars: Bradford Dillman, Chick Chandler, Donald Moffatt

Written by: Ken Pettus

Directed by: Chris Christenberry

398. Blind Hunch, *November 21, 1971*

The Cartwrights' neighbor, Sam, is murdered and the law can't find a guilty party. His brother, who was blinded in the Civil War, comes to town and, with Jamie's help, finds the man that the posse couldn't find in their four-day search.

Guest Stars: Rip Torn, Don Knight, Loretta Leversee, Charles Maxwell

Written by: John Hawkins, Robert Pirosh

Directed by: Lewis Allen

399. The Iron Butterfly, *November 28, 1971*

Lucky Hoss gets to escort the actress Lola Fairmont to Virginia City. A fallen bridge leaves them stranded. Her former boyfriend catches up with her, and she shoots him in self-defense. Hoss takes the blame for the shooting. Lola's ex-boyfriend was a senator's son, and the senator sets out to destroy the Cartwrights.

Guest Stars: Mariette Hartley, Stefan Gierasch

Written by: Harold Swanton

Directed by: Leo Penn

400. The Rattlesnake Brigade, *December 5, 1971*

The notorious Doyle gang are on their way to prison when they capture Jamie and their attorney's wife. They demand to be set free with a wagon and a team of horses. The people meet their demands, and they take Jamie and three other teenagers hostage.

Guest Stars: Neville Brand, David Sheiner, Severn Darden

Written by: Gordon T. Dawson

Directed by: William Wiard

401. Easy Come, Easy Go, *December 12, 1971*

Luke Calhoun comes to work on the Ponderosa after losing all of his money in a stock scheme. An avid card player, he turns the Ponderosa into a casino during his stay. As usual, his daughter, Meena, scares all men away in her mad search for a husband.

Guest Stars: Ann Prentiss, Dub Taylor

Written by: Jack B. Sowards

Directed by: Joseph Pevney

402. A Home for Jamie, *December 19, 1971*

Jamie's teacher shows Ben a paper that Jamie scribbled in school. It reads: Jamie Hunter, Jamie Hunter-Cartwright, Jamie H. Cartwright, Jamie Cartwright. Ben had been considering adopting Jamie for awhile. Nevada law requires that there be no traceable blood relatives. Ben had written letters to people all over the country, and no relatives came forward. But just before everything is finalized, Jamie's maternal grandfather, Paris Callahan, comes to take Jamie to Boston.

Guest Star: Will Geer

Written by: Jean Holloway

Directed by: Leo Penn

403. Warbonnet, *December 26, 1971*

Joe is stranded in the desert when his mare breaks her leg. He falls unconscious from heat stroke, and is cared for by Paiute Chief Red Cloud. After he recovers, he goes into town, where he meets Frank Ryan. Ryan, the most powerful man in town, showers Joe with hospitality. Joe feels indebted to both Red Cloud and to Frank Ryan. So when Red Cloud challenges Frank to a fight to the death, Joe tries desperately to keep peace. Fifteen years ago, Frank took Red Cloud's warbonnet. Now Red Cloud is an old man and he must regain his honor before he dies.

Guest Stars: Chief Dan George, Forrest Tucker, Linda Cristal

Written by: Arthur Heinemann, Charles Goldwad, Robert Blood

Directed by: Arthur H. Nadel

404. A Lonely Man, *January 2, 1972*

While on vacation, Hop Sing meets a shy, confused young woman named Missy. At first she keeps away, but eventually, she warms up to him. Soon he decides he wants to marry her. But there is a law prohibiting Chinese men to marry American women.

Guest Stars: *Kelly Jean Peters, Peter Hobbls*

Written by: *John Hawkins*

Directed by: *William F. Claxton*

405. Second Sight, *January 9, 1972*

Jamie is missing, and Hoss and Joe search around-the-clock. Hoss asks Judith Coleman's help – Judith was born with "second sight" or psychic ability. Hoss brings her Jamie's bandanna but she refuses to help. She's engaged to a pastor, and she has been called a witch by pastors before.

Guest Star: *Joan Hackett*

Written by: *Arthur Weingarten, Suzanne Clauser*

Directed by: *Lewis Allen*

406. Saddle Stiff, *January 16, 1972*

After Ben fires a ranch hand, he wagers with Ben that he cannot find a job and put in a decent week's work. Ben, feeling self-conscious about his age, calls his bet, and goes to work as Ben Brown. He discovers the name Ben Cartwright is hated; many folks think he's a land thief.

Guest Star: *Buddy Ebsen*

Written by:

Directed by:

407. Frenzy, *January 30, 1972*

A family of Serbian immigrants have fallen on some tough times. Back in Serbia, the husband was from a poor peasant family and his wife was from a well-off shopkeeper family. He feels she wants more than he can give her, and he cracks.

Guest Stars: *Kathleen Widdoes, Jason Karpf, Michael Pataki*

Written by: *Preston Wood, Karl Tunberg*

Directed by: *Lewis Allen*

408. Customs of the Country, *February 6, 1972*

Ben, Hoss and Joe go to Agua Santos, Mexico. Ben sends Joe to hire some help, and sends Hoss after him

Irreplaceable. Dan Blocker's untimely death in 1972 spelled the end to Bonanza.

when he doesn't return. Hoss finds Joe in "jail", where each afternoon, he's allowed to sunbathe with a harem of women. He removed his hat in church, which is desecration in Agua Santos. Hoss tries to get Joe a speedy trial, but Joe doesn't mind being jailed.

Guest Stars: Alan Oppenheimer, Pilar Seurat

Written by: Joseph Bonaduce

Directed by: Joseph Pevney

409. Shanklin, *February 13, 1972*

Shanklin, a former Confederate soldier, holds up the Ponderosa and demands $25,000. His wife and son were killed by Union soldiers, and he wants to rebuild another Confederacy. When Hoss resists, he nearly kills him. Shanklin holds everyone hostage while an incompetent doctor tries to operate on Hoss.

Guest Stars: Charles Cioffi, Woodrow Parfrey, Kara Lukas

Written by: William Felley

Directed by: Leo Penn

410. Search in Limbo, *February 20, 1972*

Ben suffers a head injury on his way to close a land deal with Sid Langley, whom he's despised for years. When he wakes up, he cannot account for one day. He learns Sid Langley had been shot during that time, and several people say they saw him at Langley's office.

Guest Stars: Albert Salmi, Lawrence Montaigne, Pamela Payton-Wright

Written by: Don Ingalls

Directed by: Leo Penn

411. He Was Only Seven, *March 5, 1972*

Joe helps his friend capture his grandson's killers.

Guest Stars: Roscoe Lee Browne, William Watson, Robert Doyle

Written by: Michael Landon

Directed by: Michael Landon

412. The Younger Brother's Younger Brother, *March 12, 1972*

The three bumbling Younger brothers are released after 12 years in prison. They fail to hold up a stage and the driver is about to arrest them when Hoss assumes the driver is the outlaw. He frees the brothers and is arrested as the Younger brothers' younger brother. The brothers release him and hold him for ransom, but the sheriff assumes they released him because he's kin. Ben pays the ransom and he and Joe go to straighten things out. When they tell the sheriff they're Hoss' family, he arrests them for being part of the Younger clan.

Guest Stars: Strother Martin, Doc Severinsen, Chuck McCann, Henry Jones

Written by: Michael Landon

Directed by: Michael Landon

413. A Place to Hide, *March 19, 1972*

Ben is visited by Rose Beckett and her daughter, Bluebird. Rose is married to outlaw Cody Ransom, wanted by Major Donahue. When New Orleans was taken in 1862, the General set up a black market. Rose wrote a letter to Washington and was convicted for sedition. Cody and his men released her from prison, and they have been running since. Rose sees Cody for the first time in 7 years, and they ask Ben's help in clearing their name. But Donahue considers capturing Ransom a personal matter.

Guest Stars: Suzanne Pleshette, Hurd Hatfield, Jodie Foster, Jon Cypher

Written by: William D. Gordon, Ward Hawkins

Directed by: Herschel Daugherty

414. A Visit to Upright, *See Lost Episodes*

415. One Ace Too Many, *April 2, 1972*

The Cartwrights go to Carson City so Ben can accept an award. Ben's lookalike, Bradley Meredith, comes to the Ponderosa, pretending to be ill. On his "deathbed", Meredith-as-Ben tries to liquidate the Ponderosa, to donate the money to the town. He actually plans to steal the cash.

Guest Stars: Greg Mullavey, Kate Jackson, William Mims

Written by: Stanley Roberts

Directed by: Lewis Allen

Season 14

416. Forever *(Two-hour episode)*, *September 12, 1972*

John Harper and his sister, Alice, move to Virginia City. John is an alcoholic gambler; each new town fails to change him. Alice is beautiful but shy; Joe falls for her immediately. Alice discovers her brother gambled away all their money; she asks him to leave. Joe and Alice become engaged. He spends much of the four-month engagement building his own Ponderosa, with Ben, Candy and Jamie's help. The happy couple has a beautiful church wedding. On the wedding night Joe gives Alice a music box that belonged to his mother. Several months later Alice says, "Looks like we're going to have to build that extra room a little sooner than we expected." Joe goes to Pa's house to pick up supplies. While he's away Alice gets a visit from her brother and a man named Damian, along with a group of henchmen headed by ape-like Mr. Hanley. John owes Damian a great deal of money, and he tells him his sister will pay off the debt. When she refuses to hand over the music box, Damian tells Hanley to kill John and Alice. Joe returns home with Candy to find his house burning. He runs into the house to find Alice and nearly dies. Overcome with grief, a bearded Joe, along with Candy, goes in search of Alice's killers. He soon finds a saloon girl playing with the music box. Michael Landon wrote this script as a showcase for Dan Blocker, but Blocker's sudden death pushed Landon into the unaltered role.

Guest Stars: Bonnie Bedelia, Roy Jenson, Andy Robinson, Larry Golden

Written by: Michael Landon

Directed by: Michael Landon

417. Heritage of Anger, *September 19, 1972*

Ben's friend is released from prison after serving a five-year term after an unfair trial. He looks forward to a new life, but finds a wife who can't accept him and business partners who aim to ruin him to avoid paying his share of the profits accumulated while he was incarcerated.

Guest Stars: Robert Lansing, Fionnuala Flanagan, Warren Kemmerling, Len Lesser

Written by: Don Ingalls

Directed by: Nick Webster

418. The Initiation, *September 26, 1972*

The only people young Ted has ever identified with are the members of his club. During the club's initiation the initiate is tied to a stake and told he'll be branded. A hot poker is prepared, but at the last moment is switched with an ice cube. Jamie goes through the initiation, and then it's his friend's turn. The friend dies during the rite. The members, especially Jamie, want to tell the sheriff what happened after an innocent man is arrested. But Ted forbids them, fearing he'll be blamed.

Guest Stars: Ronny Howard, James Chandler, Ed Bakey, Sean Kelly, Biff Elliot

Written by: Douglas Day Stewart

Directed by: Alf Kjellin

419. Riot!, *October 3, 1972*

Ben visits the Nevada State Prison to investigate prison reform. Officials hide the dying men and rotting food. For dinner they serve hearty stew instead of the usual rotten vegetables and infested grain. The prisoners riot. Their leader, Cooper, demands only better living conditions. But some prisoners demand freedom, horses and guns. They take Ben and others hostage. This is the first appearance of Griff King (Tim Matheson), a young man imprisoned for killing his abusive stepfather. He and Candy had worked together in Billings, and Griff helps his old friend free the hostages.

Guest Stars: Aldo Ray, Marco St. John

Written by: Robert Pirosh

Directed by: Lewis Allen

420. New Man, *October 10, 1972*

Griff King is paroled from prison and placed in Ben's care. He becomes an unwilling ranch hand, unable to get along with other hands. He thinks of the Ponderosa as just another prison, and his problems are compounded when he is accused of robbing the Wells Fargo station and killing a clerk.

Guest Stars: Ronny Cox, Charles Dierkop

Written by: Jack B. Sowards

Directed by: Leo Penn

421. Ambush at Rio Lobo,
October 24, 1972

Zachariah Burnside was a witness to a robbery three years ago and was responsible for jailing the criminals. Now the outlaws seek revenge by using his pregnant wife as a pawn in a stagecoach robbery. Ben tries to help, even delivering the Burnside baby.

Guest Stars: James Olson, Albert Salmi, Sian Barbara Allen, Murray MacLeod

Written by: Joel Murcott

Directed by: Nicholas Colasanto

422. The 26th Grave, *October 31, 1972*

Samuel Clemens becomes the temporary editor of Virginia City's paper. He prints a story claiming that the assayer, upon hearing of a gold strike, kills the miner and gives the claim to his cronies. The assayer sues Clemens. Clemens won't name his source and the assayer wins. After the source is murdered Clemens asks the Cartwrights to help him prove his story.

Guest Stars: Ken Howard, Dana Elcar, Stacy Keach Jr., Phil Kenneally, Walter Burke

Written by: Stanley Roberts

Directed by: Leo Penn

423. Stallion, *November 14, 1972*

Ben buys Joe a black stallion for his birthday. Joe loves the horse and is devastated when a man named Billy steals him. Billy doesn't even care when he accidentally shoots his son in a fight with Joe.

Guest Stars: Clu Gulager, Mitzi Hoag, Vincent Van Patten

Written by: Jack B. Sowards, Mort Zarcoff, Juanita Bartlett

Directed by: E.W. Swackhamer

424. The Hidden Enemy,
November 28, 1972

Miles Johnson's son has been caught in a stampede. Dr. Wills goes into a trance and the boy dies. Miles' other son vows revenge, so Clem puts Wills in jail for his own protection. He goes into a fit, and Doc Martin diagnoses him as a morphine addict, a common problem after the Civil War. Miles Johnson tries to have him prosecuted for murder. Although Wills is acquitted, he still must face his wife, his ailing son, and the rest of Virginia City.

Guest Stars: Mike Farrell, Melissa Murphy, Jason Wingreen, David Huddleston, Russell Thorsen

Written by: Stanley Roberts, Jack B. Sowards

Directed by:

425. The Sound of Sadness,
December 5, 1972

Two young boys are placed into the orphanage when they are deserted by their parents. A couple wants to adopt the older boy only, since the younger is unable to speak. The two boys run away from the orphanage. They meet up with a lonely widower named Jonathan who takes up their cause.

Guest Stars: Jack Albertson, Timothy Marshall, Dan Feronne, John Randolph, Carol Lawson

Written by: Michael Landon

Directed by: Michael Landon

426. The Bucket Dog, *December 19, 1972*

Jamie meets Tim Reilly and his dog, April. Reilly is anxious to sell April, and Jamie can't resist. The dog adores Jamie. Reilly's former employer tells Jamie April is small for her breed and a disgrace to all Irish Setters. He wants her killed before she can breed. Jamie puts April up against his best dog, Rusty, in a bird-catching contest. If April wins, Jamie keeps her. If she loses, she is killed.

Guest Stars: William Sylvester, John Zaremba, Don Knight, Ivan Bonar

Written by: John Hawkins

Directed by: William F. Claxton

427. First Love, *December 26, 1972*

Jamie has an innocent crush on his schoolteacher's wife and finds his teacher obsessively jealous.

Guest Stars: Pamela Franklin, Jordan Rhodes, Lisa Eibacher

Written by: Richard Collins

Directed by: Leo Penn

428. The Witness, *January 2, 1973*

Ben sends Candy to collect $3,000 from a widow. With documents in hand Candy checks into the hotel and eats with a woman named Kate. When he returns to his room he is knocked unconscious and the documents stolen. The thief poses as Candy, takes the money and kills the widow. Candy is arrested. The only people who can verify he was robbed are the hotel clerk and Kate; they have both left town. And Kate is the killer's wife.

Guest Stars: Sally Kemp

Written by: Joel Murcott, Arthur Heinemann

Directed by: Lewis Allen

429. The Marriage of Theodora Duffy, *January 9, 1973*

Griff and Theodora Duffy pose as husband and wife to uncover a crime ring; we find out Theodora Duffy does this for a living. Candy says it best when he says, "Will someone tell me what's going on here?" Besides the cute marriage charade scenes between Griff and Theodora Duffy, the story is impossible to follow, or maybe just too uninteresting to care.

Guest Stars: Richard Eatham, Ramon Rieri, Karen Carlson, Robert Yuro

Written by: Ward Hawkins

Directed by: William F. Claxton

430. The Hunter,
January 16, 1973

Joe is chased by a psychopathic killer, just escaped from prison. A spooky episode with almost no dialogue, but a rather odd conclusion to the 14-year legend.

Guest Stars: Tom Skerritt, Phillip Avenetti

Written by: Michael Landon

Directed by: Michael Landon

They don't make 'em like they used to! NBC produced several "Next Generation" T.V. movies, but none measured up to the original series. This photo is from "Bonanza: The Return". From left to right: Alistair MacDougall, Emily Warfield, Michael Landon Jr., Brian Lechner (front)

Joseph, get a haircut! Lorne Greene enjoyed hosting "Lorne Greene's New Wilderness" in the 80s

The Unfilmed Episodes

The following episodes were written but not filmed. All except *Bandits, Thieves and Kidnappers* are from scason 14. *Bandits, Thieves and Kidnappers* was intended for season 12 or 13. All scripts were written by Michael Landon.

A Poor Man's Treasure

Joe sees a mangy pony harnessed to a sundries cart. He notices an unhappy and thin young girl. She brings him to her unconscious, blood-covered father.

We discover Jonah Hopper fell off the wagon in a drunken spell. His daughter Ada is obedient and shy. After Jonah sobers up he and Ada leave.

A short time later, Joe discovers his gold pocket watch is gone, and Hop Sing says a set of silver salt and pepper shakers is missing. Clem arrests Jonah. Joe tells Clem to bring Ada to Emma Sheffield the dressmaker, who cares for girls to earn extra money.

Joe goes to Emma's cottage to pay for dresses Clem ordered for Ada. Ada gives Joe a brooch she "vanished" from Miss Sheffield. Ada expected Joe to be thrilled, just as her father is when she steals for him.

Joe likes and wants to help Ada. He brings her to Pastor and Mary Kirby's Sunday school. That evening, she offers Ben a gold cross and two communion cups, and Joe a brass candle snuffer and a Bible. Joe is furious, but Jamie points out Ada doesn't know right from wrong.

Joe takes Ada back to Mrs. Kirby's, and she forgives Ada. She also tells Joe that the Bible was a gift for every student. On the way back home, Joe explains to Ada that you don't have to steal presents to make people love you.

Jonah receives a suspended sentence, and comes to get Ada. He tells her to put on her dress with the pockets so she can "vanish" supplies. She runs back to the Ponderosa. Jonah goes back into his drunken state. A few days later, the Cartwrights throw a birthday party for Ada when Mary Kirby brings Jonah to the house. She says he walked all the way to church to deliver Ada's present. Jonah gives Joe half the money Joe spent on Ada's dresses. He got the money by selling the pony and wagon. He has started a new life, working as a pick and shovel man at a mine.

Barnaby

Kathy Evans is on her way to the Ponderosa when the stage's axle breaks. The driver, Ed Harrison, must get a new axle, but he also must leave Kathy alone. Three men begin watching Kathy: George Mott and his two sons, Job and Petey. A lone woman is appealing to the outlaws.

The men empty Kathy's luggage and guess from her expensive dresses that someone may be willing to pay for her return. They bring her to the Dry Creek station. When Ed Harrison tries to rescue Kathy, George kills him.

Ben gets a telegram from Kathy's father Jim which reads, "Kathy delayed...In serious trouble...Otis Barnaby on way your place...will explain...Appreciate all help..." Ben has no idea who Otis Barnaby is.

Otis Barnaby is fifty-something, average height and overweight, neatly dressed in city clothes. He lovingly savors a striped paper sack of candy. He doesn't notice Sam Casey aiming a gun at his back. Casey calls over his partner, Mitch Kline, and informs Barnaby that he has a gun pointed at him. Barnaby isn't concerned, and offers the two men candy. The outlaws are amused by the middle-aged, overweight man as they take his gold pocket watch and chain. Kline finds that Barnaby's saddlebags are loaded with money, but just as they're taking it, two shots are fired, injuring both of them. They're sure Barnaby has outriders guarding him.

After the brief distraction, Barnaby arrives at the Ponderosa. He can tell the Cartwrights were expecting more of the hired gun type. Barnaby shows Ben the letter from Kathy's father, saying that Kathy is being held for $20,000 ransom. Ben decides that Kathy would be safest if they pay the ransom, then recover the money after she's released. The letter says that only one man deliver the ransom. Joe volunteers, but Barnaby insists. The Cartwrights think it's ludicrous; Barnaby looks so helpless, and he's armed only with a small revolver. But Kathy is Barnaby's niece, and she is the only family he has.

Meanwhile, Casey and Kline, nearly recovered from their wounds, convince Link Nelson to join them in stealing the money from Barnaby's saddlebags. Now they can be prepared for his outriders.

The next morning, Barnaby leaves to deliver the ransom when he's joined by Joe and Griff. He doesn't want them along, but agrees when they promise to stay out of the way. Joe and Griff meet Casey, Kline and Nelson, who assume that they are Barnaby's outriders. Joe and Griff defeat them, then convince Barnaby to let them ride ahead. Griff hides the money so "even a packrat couldn't find it," and they leave, promising to be back in a few hours.

Casey sees Joe and Griff riding away, and tells Kline and Nelson that the outriders have gone away and "the little fat man's alone." They approach Barnaby at gunpoint, and demand the saddlebags. Barnaby says his friend hid them. Amused, Casey opens a heavy leather bag, and immediately is no longer amused. Inside the bag is an assortment of handguns, holsters and belts, and a leather folder. That is Barnaby's sample case. Barnaby sells guns for a living. Inside the leather case are posters featuring the "World Champion Fast and Fancy Revolver Shot" and the picture is unmistakeably Otis Barnaby. Nelson draws his gun, and Barnaby shoots him in the arm. The three outlaws ride away.

Meanwhile, Joe and Griff reach the Dry Creek station, and pose as Joe Shipley and Griff Towers, two saddletramps headed south. When they hear Kathy scream, they attack the three men, but are overpowered and tied up. Not long after, Barnaby arrives, carrying the saddlebags that Griff said even a packrat couldn't find. When he offers the money to the outlaws, Joe and Griff think that he just signed death warrants for all of them. They bring Kathy out, and when he sees her bruises, he says the men will have to be punished. Amused, Job and Petey draw their guns, but two shots sting their hands. Joe, Griff and the outlaws cannot believe it. When Barnaby said that he can be very persuasive, he really meant it!

The Giant Killer

It's senator election time in Virginia City. The two candidates are Judge Jacob Mallory and James Drake, a mining engineer. The issue is hydraulic mining. Mallory's slogan "A Vote For Mallory is a Vote for Jobs" implies that he's for hydraulics. James Drake is against it, he has seen is destructiveness in California.

The people think that abolishing hydraulics will put a lot of miners out of work, so James Drake is unpopular in Virginia City. He asks Ben to stand with him during his speeches. Ben is reluctant, but after Joe promises to take care of the ranch, he agrees.

In Drake's next speech, he introduces his wife, Nora, the daughter of Jonah Watson, who is remembered as a hero. Drake takes full advantage of that in his speech, saying "...I'm sure most of you know who Jonah Watson was...He pioneered this country around here...He believed in it...he belived in its future...and so do I." Just then, a bullet hits Drake in the leg.

Nora says James hasn't smiled since the campaign began. Just when they begin to argue, Ben and Joe tell Drake that the man who shot him got away. Drake doesn't care; he's only thinking about the campaign. Joe walks Nora back to the hotel. Nora tells Joe that her father, was no hero; he was actually a whiskey lover and womanizer. She's tired of her husband talking about him, and she's tired of the campaign.

Ben is furious at Drake's decision to go to Rimfire mining camp, telling him, "They'll cut you up for dogmeat." But Drake points out the vote is evenly divided; Mallory has all the miners and he has all the farmers and ranchers. Mallory expresses his sympathy about Drake's gunshot wound. He offers to call off his campaign if Drake does the same, but he refuses. Nora wants to leave James. She agrees to go to Rimfire only as Jonah Watson's daughter, not as James' wife.

Ben gives Dusty a letter requesting $2,000 in campaign funds and tells him to deliver it to the Merchants Bank in Reno. He is to leave the next morning. Joe feels Ben should send some men along with Dusty for protection. Ben disagrees, saying he chose Dusty for the job because no one would suspect he is carrying all that money.

The next day, Ben, Drake and Nora arrive in Rimfire. Tremble, Drake's campaign manager, tells Drake that the miners tear down his posters every night. He also tells Ben that all the hotel rooms are taken, probably by Mallory. Snyder, a local miner, tells Drake aif he's really the miners' friend, he should camp along with them.

The next day, Drake is prepared to make his speech, but only one miner is there. The rest are drinking at the saloon courtesy of Judge Mallory. Drake cancels his speech and goes to the saloon with Ben, Tremble, and Nora. He confronts Judge Mallory on hydraulic mining, igniting the miners' fury. Drake explains that he's not a politician; he's a mining engineer, and shows the callouses he got from swinging a sledgehammer. He bets a local miner named Bull that he can out-drill him in a double-jack drilling race. Bull agrees that if Drake wins, he will vote for him.

Drake very predictably wins the race. Ben gets a telegram from Dusty; he was waylaid on the trail and robbed of the $2,000. Drake finds the campsite had been wrecked. He blames the vandalism and his bullet wound on the miners who want to hide the truth.

But the truth dawns on Ben. Jim was the only one who knew Dusty was carrying that money. He pieces that together with the suspiciously minor gunshot wound, the mysteriously occupied hotel, the campsite wreck, and the unhappy wife. Ben threatens to create an ugly scene if Drake doesn't sign a paper withdrawing from the race. Tremble left town earlier, right after he signed a confession.

Bandits, Thieves and Kidnappers

Hoss and Joe are taking care of business in town when they meet up with Sam, a reporter for the Virginia City Enterprise and a rather undesirable man. Hoss greets him with a simple "Afternoon, Sam." Sam replies, "Yes, it certainly is. Since the sun rises on the left and sets on the right and since it now occupies the quadrant on the right, it is probably afternoon."

Joe reminds Hoss that they have a big day tomorrow, post holes to dig and wire to stretch. Hoss wants to stay in town and relax, so he promises Joe he'll be back early, and Joe heads home. Hoss goes to the saloon, where Sam cons him into treating him to the finest bottle of whiskey.

Hoss is approached by Cal and Jeb Murphy, two bumbling aspiring outlaws. They try to rob him, but he doesn't have any money. Then they try to steal his horse, before they realize that his horse ran away. They consider the idea of Hoss writing them a check, but then they remember they held up someone who wrote them a bad check. Finally, they decide to kidnap Hoss, figuring that someone that big has to be worth something. They bring him back to their cabin, where their sister, Grace, is cooking dinner. At first, she is opposed to the kidnapping idea; she's tired of "feedin'

Dan Blocker appeared with Lorne Greene in a production of "The Greatest Glory" at Sul Ross in 1966. Here, they pose with Freda Gibson-Powell and Blocker's friend and former classmate, Dennis Reid. Photo courtesy Sul Ross State University.

all the scum and riff-raff" they bring in. But she develops a crush on Hoss. She brings him a delicious bowl of stew, but that doesn't change Hoss' mind about her two brothers. He plans on wiping the floor with them. She begs him not to, saying that she's been trying to set them straight. She asks him to remain kidnapped for two or three days, and then ask the trial judge to give them two or three months of hard labor. Hoss thinks about the alternative: digging post holes and stretching wire, and suddenly being kidnapped doesn't sound so bad. And he loves her cooking. He agrees to the plan on two conditions, if Grace brings him another bowl of stew, and if he can write a note to Pa. Meanwhile, Cal and Jeb write their own note, and deliver both notes to the Ponderosa.

Joe and Ben laugh at the two letters. Joe reads Cal and Jeb's letter which says, "If you don't pay the ransom of $20, we will do him in." Ben reads Hoss' letter: "Dear Pa, Don't worry, this should all be over in a few days. I am comfortable and the food is good. Your loving son, Hoss." They're both sure that Hoss just rode to Reno to escape digging post holes. They

A man and his beer. Dan at one of his hotel room parties during an appearance at Sul Ross. Photo courtesy Sul Ross State University.

than once. They're strangers in town, otherwise they would know "that corpulent Cartwright" is worth more than $70. They are hiding in an abandoned cabin in the mountains, since Hoss wrote that he's comfortable, and there is a woman with them, which explains the good food. Clem warns him that he prints any of that in the Territorial Enterprise, he'll throw him in jail.

Joe pays the ransom, and soon Clem spots a hand grabbing the envelope from under the rock. He follows Jeb, undetected, but he doesn't know that Sam is following him. Cal and Jeb return to the cabin, thrilled about the $50 and thinking about their next ransom note. Sam knocks at the door. Grace tries to turn him away, until he says he's a reporter for the Territorial Enterprise trying to get information on the Hoss Cartwright kidnapping. Cal and Jeb ask him in; they think they'll be famous and respected when their story is published. Cal brings Sam down to the cellar to talk to Hoss, but Sam is the last person Hoss wants to see. Sam is just about to leave when Cal stops him. Sam knows too much, and now Cal has to kill him. But Grace has developed a crush on Sam, and insists that they lock him in the cellar with Hoss. Cal and Jeb write another ransom note, this time for $100. Ben, Joe and Clem lead a posse toward the cabin.

stop laughing when Jamie tells them that Hoss' horse just wandered in. Joe agrees to deliver the $20 ransom, thinking he might be able to see the man who picks it up. He and Jamie put the envelope under a rock. They stay for three hours, but they don't notice a hand grabbing the envelope from under the bushes.

Cal and Jeb are thrilled over the $20, and figure if someone was willing to pay that, they would be willing to pay much more, maybe as high as $50! At first, Grace insists that they free Hoss, but then she's thrilled with the idea of keeping him for a few days.

Ben wakes up on the living room couch the next morning; he had been waiting up for Hoss all night. He's furious when he finds another ransom note, this time demanding $50. He decides to pay it, but this time he will bring in the law. Clem decides that Joe will pay the ransom and leave the rest to him.

After Ben and Joe leave Clem's office, Sam, who had been listening through a jailhouse crack, walks in. He says he has come up with a few conclusions. The kidnappers are amateurs, since collecting the ransom is the most dangerous part, and they're doing it more

Sam is busily writing in the root cellar about the daring escape he's planning. Hoss says that's ridiculous – as soon as Ben pays the ransom, the Murphy's will free him. Sam informs him that Ben did pay the ransom, twice. Hoss pounds on the door and tells them that the ransom was paid and he should go free. When no one is watching, Hoss grabs the latchstring on the door, but Cal fires four shots which all narrowly miss Hoss. As Jeb leads them back down to the cellar, he tells them he wrote another ransom note, this time for $100. Sam convinces him to demand $10,000 and even agrees to compose the note for him.

The posse stops a mile from the cabin and continues the rest of the way on foot, while Sam finishes the four-page ransom note. Cal agrees to let Sam deliver it. Jeb goes out to get him a horse, while the posse watches him. Suddenly, a shot is fired from the other direction, from Jamie's rifle; Ben did not know he had come along. Cal and Jeb start shooting from inside the cabin, and the posse shoots back, breaking lamps, dishes, mirrors, and just about everything else. Ben demands to see Hoss, so they send him out to show he's okay. He walks back in and, ignoring the rifle in Cal's hands, gives the mandatory speech. "Cal, Jeb, This is how it ends. And this is how it's always gonna end. Not in the big time, or the big money, but right here. With somebody waitin' close by to put a bullet in you, or a rope around your neck."

Three Lost Episodes

These three episodes are no longer shown in the United States. The syndication rights are owned by Pat Robertson's Family Channel, and they have deemed them inappropriate. *The Pursued* deals with the now-abolished Mormon practice of polygamy, and *A Visit to Upright* features a nude painting, something you'd see by the hundreds in any art museum.

Thanks to Valerie Martin Arvelo, of the Canary Islands, who is fortunate enough to own these rare episodes (in PAL format and dubbed into Spanish), and was kind enough to provide these detailed summaries. Valerie writes wonderful *Bonanza* fiction; check out my "plugs" at the end of the Ponderosa Ranch chapter for more details!

239. The Pursued (Part I), *October 2, 1966*

The Cartwrights go to Beehive to buy horses from Mormon rancher Heber Clawson. The townspeople are throwing mud at Clawson, who doesn't react. Wealthy ranch owner Grant Carbo intervenes. The Cartwrights later meet Clawson's two wives, Susana and Elizabeth. Elizabeth is pregnant.

Hoss later says he had no idea Clawson wasn't normal. Ben defends the Mormon principle of polygamy (now abolished) by explaining 600 of them were killed when they were expelled from their land, and they would have vanished if not for polygamy. Besides, Ben reminds them, polygamy existed in the Old Testament.

The wives take dinner to the men. Heber suggests they borrow a couple of hands from Carbo. Susana gives a look that says there's a problem between she and Carbo. Ben and Hoss leave Joe in charge of the roundup, and they head home.

On Sunday, Susana and Elizabeth want to go to church. Heber is afraid the new pastor won't welcome them. The ladies win. The sermon is a diatribe against Mormons, and Joe and the Mormons leave. The pastor says Mormons hire killers and no one is safe with them in town. Carbo says Susana is a victim and must be rescued; he is obviously interested in her.

Carbo forces his way into the Mormon home and tries to convince Susana to have her husband sell him the ranch and stay with him. Susana pushes him away. Elizabeth returns and realizes something is wrong and convinces Susana to tell Heber, who confronts Carbo. Susana fetches Joe. When he gets to town, Heber and Carbo are fighting. Heber is winning, but Carbo goes for his gun. Joe shoots it out of his hand. Joe holding his gun on anyone who interferes with the fight, which Heber wins.

The townspeople are stirred against the Mormons and convinced Joe is a hired killer, like the pastor described. A few days later, Heber goes to buy supplies and the shopkeeper won't extend credit. Susana finds people won't even say good morning.

The pastor tries to convince the women they are an affront to God. Heber throws the pastor out.

Joe, Susana and Heber are herding horses when Carbo's men cause a stampede. Joe confronts Carbo's foreman, the foreman draws his gun, and Joe kills him in self defense. Heber says they must leave. Joe tries to convince them otherwise, but they're determined. The two women go ahead in the wagon, while Joe and Heber stay behind to fight off the townspeople. They burn the barn and house, and Joe and Heber escape through the smokescreen. Carbo and the Pastor decide to let them go for now – they'll have to cross the desert and will be easier to catch later.

Guest Stars: Eric Fleming, Dina Merrill, Lois Nettleton

240. The Pursued (Part II),
October 9, 1966

Joe and Heber find the women on the side of the road. Elizabeth is in late pregnancy, and she's exhausted. Heber says he wants to go back to Salt Lake City to raise his child Mormon. Then the townspeople start closing in. The women drive the wagon quickly, and Joe and Heber ride behind, closely pursued by about twelve people. When the townspeople begin to fire, they take cover behind rocks. Susana wants to reason with Carbo, but the others won't let her. Elizabeth goes into labor.

Carbo is only after Susana, but the pastor rants about eternal salvation. The Mormons and Joe take to the road again with the townspeople in pursuit.

Joe catches up with Hoss and Ben. They start a horse stampede which slows the pursuers. Several of the pursuers have been shot and those left are losing nerve. The pastor says he's going to talk to the women. Carbo is only along to get Susana. The pastor thought Carbo was interested in the women's salvation.

Elizabeth and Susana are in the wagon; Elizabeth is having contractions. Susana asks Heber if they'll always live like this. Heber says one day the world will be a perfect place without hatred. Then Carbo shoots him in the back, killing him. Carbo grabs Susana by the hair and says he always gets what he wants. Joe appears, gun drawn, and tells Carbo to leave. Carbo draws and Joe kills him.

The pastor appears and wants the Cartwrights arrested. But two of Carbo's men say Carbo murdered Heber and Joe shot in self-defense. Joe accuses the pastor of being responsible for the deaths. The pastor rants about saving souls, and Ben says he should look to his own soul.

Elizabeth has trouble giving birth, and Joe rides for a doctor. He returns with the doctor, but it's in vain. Elizabeth dies after giving birth.

Another pastor with his wife appear. They offer to look after the baby and give Susana a temporary home. Susana is suspicious, but this pastor and his wife are good people. As they leave, Hoss points out that there are good people in the world.

Guest Stars: Same as above

414. A Visit to Upright, *March 26, 1972*

Joe and Hoss acquire a part share of a saloon in Upright. They go there with Jamie, to take possession and sell their share. When they arrive they see a thriving saloon, and they walk in and introduce themselves. To their disgust, their saloon is across the street – a dilapidated, dirty shack. There is a barmaid, and one regular customer, an Italian. Hoss and Joe are suspicious when they receive offers of far more than the saloon's value. They discover that the deceased owner hid a fortune somewhere on the premises, and from there on the search is on! Walls are ripped out at night, the floor is dug up. All through this, the Italian customer comes every day to look at the picture of a nude woman behind the bar.

Meanwhile, back in Carson City, Ben is in the middle of delicate business negotiations with a very strict, moralistic lady. She hears that two of Ben's son's are running a saloon, and the deal is off unless the saloon is sold by a specific time. Ben sends several irate telegrams to Joe and Hoss, but Joe just grins and says that Pa doesn't understand the situation.

The barmaid is anxious to get paid, and as there's no money in the kitty. They pay her off with the picture of the nude woman, which isn't really what she wanted, so she throws it away in the street.

The Italian customer deserts them, and they ask him why he never comes to the saloon anymore. He says he used to go to look at that magnificent Titian hanging behind the bar, but now it's gone. Joe and Hoss had no idea that painting was a work of art worth a lot of money. That was the hidden fortune they were searching for.

Meanwhile, Ben arrives at Upright with about half an hour to spare to meet the deadline for selling the saloon. The sheriff arrives and says the painting was stolen from a train years ago, and that it belongs to a museum, and Hoss and Joe can't sell it.

So Joe and Hoss realize they'd better sell the saloon, because Ben has one of his 'looks' on his face – so they ask for offers. Before people were offering $1,000 or more – suddenly, no one is interested! In the end they have to give it away.

Guest Stars: Alan Oppenheimer, Loretta Swit, Anne Seymour

The Ponderosa Ranch

Yes, the Ponderosa Ranch really exists! Each year, an increasing number of *Bonanza* fans head to Incline Village, Nevada, where they can see in person the big, beautiful ranch that used to grace their television sets every Sunday night at 9:00, and continues to do so in reruns. This is all thanks to Bill Anderson, a former part-time contractor and, in his words, "a gutsy sort of guy," and his wife, Joyce.

Bill and Joyce Anderson first came to Incline Village, Nevada in the early 1960's, when *Bonanza* had been on the air almost four years. Bill's job at the time was supply a large development company on the north shore of Lake Tahoe with equipment necessary to carry out their operation. As a sideline, the Andersons opened a riding stable to assist in the development company's vision to boost recreation in the area. They also

The Ponderosa Ranch in Incline Village Nevada, where many episodes were filmed after 1967

stabled the horses used in the *Bonanza* filmings. Tourists were flocking to the lake area, Anderson found, but after talking with some fans, he realized that people were walking away disappointed. They were convinced, from the picture of the map each week, that they had found the Ponderosa Ranch, but there was no ranch to be found.

"It always bothered me that tourists here at the lake were forever hunting around for a place where the Ponderosa Ranch might have been, and they couldn't find it," Bill Anderson explained. "They wanted to see, in person, the beautiful, sprawling ranch they saw weekly on their television screens. It had to be somewhere nearby, because they had seen its location on the famous 'burning map' each Sunday evening." He approached NBC, as well as Lorne Greene, Dan Blocker and Michael Landon with his idea, and with the help of their financial backing, Anderson headed up the operation to "make a legend come alive". An ambitious construction program was launched, and in the summer of 1967, the gates of the Ponderosa Ranch swung open to the public for the first time. Bill Anderson's prediction that "people will come from all over the world to see it" certainly came true when more than a quarter-million visitors came through the gates. "It overwhelmed us," Anderson recalls, "but we did what had to be done...we took care of them." And that's what Bill and Joyce Anderson, together with a highly trained staff of "Ponderosa Ranchhands" have been doing ever since!

The early days of the Ponderosa Ranch were exciting ones, nearly all the filming from 1967 to *Bonanza*'s end in 1973 was done on location at the ranch. On any given day, a visitor could catch a glimpse of their favorite Cartwright, and stood a good chance of getting an autograph. After production of *Bonanza* stopped in 1973, the Andersons devoted themselves to retaining the original excitement. The Cartwright ranch house, which is the starting point of the tour, is painstakingly kept exactly the way the millions of fans remember it each week on their television screens. Outside is the massive Ponderosa pine house, the hitching post, the corrals, the barn, the workshop, all in a backdrop of the Sierra Mountains and Lake Tahoe. Inside is Hop Sing's kitchen, with the table all set for Ben and the boys, the Cartwrights' hats and jackets hanging near the front door, and all the furnishings just as they appeared.

In addition to the ranch house tour, visitors can enjoy the old west town, where, everywhere you look, you find a reminder of the way it was when Ben and the boys rode into Virginia City. There's an old gallows prominently displayed in the center of town, a reminder to the bad guys that a life of crime will give them a one-way ticket to boot hill. Also in town are many shops, the General Store, the Silver Dollar Saloon, the early west museum featuring memorabilia of the period, hundreds of carriages, wagons, antiques, and early farm equipment, the Pettin' Farm, Hoss's Mystery Mine, charcoaled Hossburgers, the famous Ponderosa church, and much more!

Special Attractions

A Legal 'n Proper Ponderosa Wedding

Bonanza fans can have a most unforgettable wedding at the Church of the Ponderosa, an authentic 1870 country church (seating capacity 125) performed by the Church of the Ponderosa Minister, all legal 'n proper, of course. For $150 (fee at press time) the happy couple can enjoy use of the church and minister, 20 free guests ($4.00 per person over 20 guests), tour of the Cartwright Ranch House, an old-fashioned photo of the couple, a vintage limousine ride, and bride's changing room. Optional services include floral arrangements, photography and champagne. For more information and reservations, write to: Church of the Ponderosa, 100 Ponderosa Ranch Road, Incline Village, NV 89451 or call Bill or Joyce Anderson at (702) 831-0691 or FAX (702) 831-0113. Weddings are performed all through the ranch's season, from May 1 to October 31.

Filming a Virginia City scene

The Western Style Bonanza Deep-Pit Bar-B-Que Party

For convention groups of 100 or more, the Ponderosa Ranch offers a unique experience with the Western Style *Bonanza* Deep-Pit Bar-B-Que Party. The idea started shortly after the ranch opened its doors in 1967, when Bill and Joyce Anderson were approached by several convention planners who asked if the ranch could be made available for private parties. Bill recalled that many years ago, Basque sheepherders who moved their sheep through the Nevada High Country and the Sierra range, used a deep-pit cooking method to prepare their meals. Before leaving camp at sunup, the shepherds would place the coals from the previous night's fire into a pit. They then wrapped chunks of lamb in wine-soaked cloths, placed them on the bed of coals, covered it with moistened leaves and dirt, and left the meat to slowly cook throughout the day. When they returned at nightfall, all they had to do was un-wrap the meat and enjoy a mouthwatering meal. The Andersons have adapted this age-old cooking technique to their Deep Pit Bar-B-Que parties with one exception, succulent Nevada beef has replaced the lamb. Large chunks of meat are wrapped in cheesecloth and burlap that has been soaked in Burgundy wine and spices, placed over mahogany coals in a deep pit, covered with sand, and allowed to cook for five to six hours. The result? A sumptuous meal that's not to be forgot-ten! Put it together with three and a half hours of kickin' up your heels and tappin' your toes to the tunes of a live western band, and the untapped flow of "Mountain Dew", the name for all drinks served at the Ponderosa, and you and your convention group will have the evening of your lives!

The Haywagon Breakfast

For the best possible way to see the Ponderosa Ranch, climb aboard the haywagon for a ride through the beautiful tall timber, then settle down at the hearty, all-you-can-eat wagon camp breakfast. Savor Ben's scrambled eggs, Hop Sing's sausage, flapjacks, coffee and juice, all overlooking breathtaking Lake Tahoe. Haywagons depart Memorial Day weekend through Labor Day weekend, 8:00-9:30AM daily. Ranch admission is included.

An Old Tin Cup, The Official Souvenir of the Ponderosa Ranch

When the Andersons were preparing to open the ranch doors for the first time back in 1967 after an eternity of painstaking planning, they realized that there was one detail that had not been planned, an official souvenir. After some thought, they got their inspiration from Lorne Greene's hit recording entitled "An Old Tin Cup". But where were they going to find a tin cup manufacturer in 1967? After a nationwide search, Bill Anderson found the Schlueter Manufacturing Company of St. Louis, a firm that hadn't produced any great quantity of tin cups since the Civil War, but still had their manufacturing machinery in working order. Anderson contracted the firm for an initial order of 35 dozen, and they were subsequently decorated with a Ponderosa Ranch decal.

From such modest beginnings, the tin cup has grown to over 100,000 orders, making the Ponderosa Ranch the largest user of tin cups since the Civil War. Now, the cups come photo-engraved with a picture of the ranch house, the Cartwrights and the Ponderosa Brand.

A Few Plugs:

The Bonanza Mailing List on the Web

Yes Pa, the Cartwrights have gone on-line! There is a wonderful mailing list on the Internet where diehard Bonanza fans meet in Cyberspace to discuss – well, you name it! Warning: we are a lively group, so be prepared for LOTS of email! Signing up is easy. Just go to:

http://home.earthlink.net/~deirdre/index.html/

and click on "join Bonanza mailing list"!

The Michael Landon Internet Fan Club

This is a must-join club, where you'll be treated to rare photos, exclusive interviews, and many other surprises! Join at:

http://members.aol.com/cadetteel/index.htm

While you're at these sites, check out the other links too. New sites are always being added!

The Bear Family CD set

Several times I mentioned the Bear Family set of CDs covering most of the *Bonanza* recordings. I've been told this set is available from Tower Records Online or CD Universe.

Bonanza Fiction

Valerie Martin Arvelo (of the Canary Islands) writes wonderful *Bonanza* fiction. For more information, email her at martin@hello-net.es, or you can contact her through the *Bonanza* mailing list mentioned above!

Season One
1. A Rose for Lotta (pilot)
2. The Sun Mountain Herd
3. The Newcomers
4. The Paiute War
5. Enter Mark Twain
6. The Julia Bulette Story
7. The Saga of Annie O'Toole
8. The Phillip Diedeshiemer Story
9. Mr. Henry TP Comstock
10. The Magnificent Adah
11. The Truckee Strip
12. The Hanging Posse
13. Vendetta
14. The Sisters
15. The Last Hunt
16. El Toro Grande
17. The Outcast
18. House Divided
19. The Gunmen
20. The Fear Merchants
21. The Spanish Grant
22. Blood on the Land
23. Desert Justice
24. The Stranger
25. Escape to the Ponderosa
26. The Avenger
27. The Last Trophy
28. San Francisco
29. Bitter Water
30. Feet Of Clay
31. Dark Star
32. Death at Dawn

Season Two
33. Showdown
34. The Mission
35. Badge Without Honor
36. The Mill
37. The Hopefuls
38. Denver McKee
39. Day of Reckoning
40. The Abduction
41. Breed of Violence
42. The Last Viking
43. The Trail Gang
44. The Savage
45. Silent Thunder
46. The Ape
47. The Blood Line
48. The Courtship
49. The Spitfire
50. The Bride
51. Bank Run
52. The Fugitive
53. Vengeance
54. Tax Collector
55. The Rescue
56. The Dark Gate
57. The Duke
58. Cut Throat Junction
59. The Gift
60. The Rival
61. The Infernal Machine
62. Thunderhead Swindle
63. The Secret

64. The Dream Riders
65. Elizabeth, My Love
66. Sam Hill

Season Three
67. The Smiler
68. Springtime
69. The Honor of Cochise
70. The Lonely House
71. The Burma Rarity
72. Broken Ballad
73. The Many Faces of Gideon Flinch
74. The Friendship
75. The Countess
76. The Horse Breaker
77. Day of the Dragon
78. The Frenchman
79. The Tin Badge
80. Gabrielle
81. Land Grab
82. The Tall Stranger
83. The Lady from Baltimore
84. The Ride
85. The Storm
86. The Auld Sod
87. Gift of Water
88. The Jackknife
89. The Guilty
90. The Wooing of Abigail Jones
91. The Lawmaker
92. Look to the Stars
93. The Gamble
94. The Crucible
95. Inger, My Love
96. Blessed Are They
97. The Dowry
98. The Long Night
99. The Mountain Girl
100. The Miracle Worker

Season Four
101. The Firstborn
102. The Quest
103. The Artist
104. A Hot Day For a Hanging
105. The Deserter
106. The Way Station
107. The War Comes to Washoe
108. Knight Errant
109. The Beginning
110. The Deadly Ones
111. Gallagher's Sons
112. The Decision
113. The Good Samaritan
114. The Jury
115. The Colonel
116. Song in the Dark
117. Elegy for a Hangman
118. Half a Rogue
119. The Last Haircut
120. Marie, My Love
121. The Hayburner
122. The Actress
123. A Stranger Passed This Way
124. The Way of Aaron
125. A Woman Lost

126. Any Friend of Walter's
127. Mirror of a Man
128. My Brother's Keeper
129. Five into the Wind
130. The Saga of Whizzer McGee
131. Thunder Man
132. Rich Man, Poor Man
133. The Boss
134. Little Man Ten Feet Tall

Season Five
135. She Walks in Beauty
136. A Passion for Justice
137. Rain From Heaven
138. Twilight Town
139. The Toy Soldier
140. A Question of Strength
141. Calamity Over the Comstock
142. Journey Remembered
143. The Quality of Mercy
144. The Waiting Game
145. The Legacy
146. Hoss and the Leprechauns
147. The Prime of Life
148. The Lila Conrad Story
149. Ponderosa Matador
150. My Son, My Son
151. Alias Joe Cartwright
152. The Gentleman From New Orleans
153. The Cheating Game
154. Bullet for a Bride
155. King of the Mountain
156. Love Me Not
157. The Pure Truth
158. No Less A Man
159. Return to Honor
160. The Saga of Muley Jones
161. The Roper
162. A Pink Cloud Comes from Old Cathay
163. The Companeros
164. Enter Thomas Bowers
165. The Dark Past
166. The Pressure Game
167. Triangle
168. Walter and the Outlaws

Season Six
169. Invention of a Gunfighter
170. The Hostage
171. The Wild One
172. Thanks for Everything
173. Logan's Treasure
174. The Scapegoat
175. A Dime's Worth of Glory
176. Square Deal Sam
177. Between Heaven and Earth
178. Old Sheba
179. A Man to Admire
180. The Underdog
181. A Knight to Remember
182. The Saga of Squaw Charlie

183. The Flapjack Contest
184. The Far, Far Better Thing
185. Woman of Fire
186. The Ballerina
187. The Flannel-Mouth Gun
188. Ponderosa Birdman
189. The Search
190. The Deadliest Game
191. Once A Doctor
192. Right is the Fourth R
193. Hound Dog
194. The Trap
195. Dead and Gone
196. A Good Night's Rest
197. To Own the World
198. Lothario Larkin
199. The Return
200. The Jonah
201. The Spotlight
202. Patchwork Man

Season Seven
203. The Debt
204. The Dilemma
205. The Brass Box
206. The Other Son
207. The Lonely Runner
208. Devil on Her Shoulder
209. Found Child
210. The Meredith Smith
211. Mighty is the Word
212. The Strange One
213. The Reluctant Rebel
214. Five Sundowns to Sunup
215. A Natural Wizard
216. All Ye His Saints
217. A Dublin Lad
218. To Kill a Buffalo
219. Ride the Wind Pt1
220. Ride the Wind Pt2
221. Destiny's Child
222. Peace Officer
223. The Code
224. Three Brides for Hoss
225. The Emperor Norton
226. Her Brother's Keeper
227. The Trouble with Jamie
228. Shining in Spain
229. The Genius
230. The Unwritten Commandment
231. Big Shadows on the Land
232. The Fighters
233. Home from the Sea
234. The Last Mission
235. A Dollars Worth of Trouble

Season Eight
236. Something Hurt, Something Wild
237. Horse of a Different Hue
238. A Time to Step Down
239. The Pursued Pt1
240. The Pursued Pt2
241. To Bloom for Thee
242. Credit for a Kill

243. Four Sisters from Boston
244. Old Charlie
245. Ballad of the Ponderosa
246. The Oath
247. A Real Nice Friendly Little Town
248. The Bridegroom
249. Tommy
250. A Christmas Story
251. Ponderosa Explosion
252. Justice
253. A Bride for Buford
254. Black Friday
255. The Unseen Wound
256. Journey to Terror
257. Amigo
258. A Woman in the House
259. Judgment at Red Creek
260. Joe Cartwright, Detective
261. Dark Enough to See the Stars
262. The Deed & the Dilemma
263. The Prince
264. A Man Without Land
265. Napoleon's Children
266. The Wormwood Cup
267. Clarissa
268. Maestro Hoss
269. The Greedy Ones

Season Nine
270. Second Chance
271. Sense of Duty
272. The Conquistadores
273. Judgment at Olympus
274. Night of Reckoning
275. False Witness
276. The Gentle Ones
277. Desperate Passage
278. The Sure Thing
279. Showdown at Tahoe
280. Six Black Horses
281. Check Rein
282. Justice Deferred
283. The Gold Detector
284. The Trackers
285. A Girl Named George
286. The Thirteenth Man
287. The Burning Sky
288. The Price Of Salt
289. Blood Tie
290. The Crime of Johnny Mule
291. The Late Ben Cartwright
292. Star Crossed
293. Trouble Town
294. Commitment at Angelus
295. A Dream to Dream
296. In Defense of Honor
297. To Die in Darkness
298. The Bottle Fighter
299. The Arrival of Eddie
300. The Stronghold
301. Pride of a Man
302. A Severe Case of Matrimony

Guest Star Index

A

Bonanza Theme from "Welcome to the Ponderosa"

Songs and stories of the American West performed by a master.
"Ringo" made it all the way to number one!

We chased lady luck 'til we
  finally struck Bonanza
With a gun and a rope and
  a hatful of hope we planted
  our family tree
We got a hold of a pot full of
  gold - Bonanza
With a horse and a saddle
  and a rakeful of cattle, how
  rich could a fella be?

On this land, we put our
  brand
Cartwright is the name
Fortune smiled the day we
  filed
The Ponderosa claim

Here in the West, we're living
  in the best Bonanza
If anyone fights any one of
  us - he's gotta fight with me
Hoss and Joe and Adam
  know
Every rock and pine
No one works, fights or eats
Like those boys of mine

Here we stand in the middle of a grand Bonanza
With a gun and a rope and a hatful of hope we planted our family tree
We got a hold of a potful of gold - Bonanza
With a houseful of friends where the rainbow ends, how rich could a fella be?

On this land, we put our brand
Cartwright is the name
Fortune smiled the day we filed
The Ponderosa claim

Here in the west we're living in the best Bonanza
With the friendliest sprite and the stubbornest man
That ever set foot in the promised land
And we're happier than them all
That's why we call it Bonanza!

And Now For Something Completely Different . . .

This song was originally tacked onto the end of *Bonanza's* first episode, "A Rose for Lotta". Thankfully, it was cut before the episode aired, otherwise *Bonanza* might not have made it past September 12, 1959.

If you're familiar with the last scene of "Lotta", Ben, Hoss and Joe do the singing while Adam passionately kisses Lotta. You can see it on a variety of specials, most recently "Back to Bonanza", an excellent retrospective.

Apparently, Pa never heard of political correctness!

(Little Joe solo): I've got a flair for women everywhere - Bonanza!
(Hoss solo): Bonanza! (Barks and howls)
(All three): I'm not afraid of any pretty maid - Bonanza! Bonanza!
But when I give a kiss to any little miss
She'll learn a lot from me
(Ben solo): I'm not afraid of any pretty maid - Bonanza!
(All three): Bonanza!
When I give a kiss to any little miss
She'll learn a lot from me
Hair of brown, hair of gold
I take what I see
We're not a one to saddle up and run - Bonanza! Bonanza!
Any one of us who starts a little fuss
Knows he can count on me
One for four, four for one
This we guarantee
We got a right to pick a little fight - Bonanza! Bonanza!
If anyone fights any one of us
He's gotta fight with me!

Pernell Roberts only appears for one song on this album. You haven't lived until you've heard Dan Blocker sing "Deck the Halls"! Available on the Bear Family set.